THE **NEXT POPE**

THE NEXT POPE

*A Behind-the-Scenes Look at How the
Successor to John Paul II Will Be Elected
and Where He Will Lead the Church*

PETER HEBBLETHWAITE

Revised and updated by
MARGARET HEBBLETHWAITE

HarperSanFrancisco
A Division of HarperCollinsPublishers

HarperCollins books may be purchased for educational, business, or sales promotional use. For information please write: Special Markets Department, HarperCollins Publishers Inc., 10 East 53rd Street, New York, NY 10022.

HarperCollins Web site: http://www.harpercollins.com

HarperCollins®, ®, and HarperSanFrancisco™ are trademarks of HarperCollins Publishers, Inc.

FIRST EDITION

Based on a design by Ralph Fowler

Library of Congress Cataloging-in-Publication Data
Hebblethwaite, Peter.
    The Next Pope : a behind-the-scenes look at how the successor to John Paul II will be elected and where he will lead the Church / Peter Hebblethwaite; revised and updated by Margaret Hebblethwaite.—1st ed.
        p. cm.
    Includes bibliographical references and index.
    ISBN 0–06–063777–3
    1. Papacy—History—20th century. 2. Catholic Church.
Collegium Cardinalium—History—20th century. 3. John Paul II, Pope, 1920– 4. Catholic Church—History—1965– I. Hebblethwaite, Margaret. II. Title.

BX1805.H39 2000
262'.135—dc21   99-058506

05 06 07 08 ❖RRD(H) 10 9 8 7 6 5 4 3

CONTENTS

CONTENTS

A section of photographs begins on page 90.

PREFACE

My husband, Peter Hebblethwaite, died on December 18, 1994, and was buried on December 23, a couple of hours after the advance copies of the first British edition of *The Next Pope* arrived in our hall. It could be seen as a token reminder that there is life after death. The U.S. edition came out some weeks later and included a final, stop-press chapter covering not only the pope's "definitive" dismissal of women priests, *Ordinatio Sacerdotalis*, but also the new cardinals created at the consistory of November 26, 1994. Peter kept working up to the end.

In one sense not a great deal has happened since then. The leading candidates of 1994–95 are still around: there have been no high-profile deaths. On the other hand, they are quite a bit older, and a man who looked a plausible successor at the age of sixty-seven is no longer such a convincing candidate at the age of nearly seventy-three (Cardinal

Martini, for example). There has been one more consistory, in February 1998, giving us twenty new cardinals, out of whom we might regard a number as *papabili* (or papal candidates): Castrillón Hoyos, Rivera Carrera, Rouco Varela, Schönborn, and Tettamanzi. Of course these judgments can be argued over, and that is the point of this book.

With regard to papal policies—which prime the conclave to decide which way the Church should move next—there has been "yet more of the same," as Peter predicted. The last five years have brought us more arguments over the appointment of bishops (in Chur and Vienna, Evreux and Santiago de Chile), more dogmatic encyclicals (*Evangelium Vitae*, for example), more investigations of theologians (even the excommunication of one of them, Tissa Balasuriya), more calls to order (*Ad Tuendam Fidem*, to punish dissent, and *Apostolos Suos*, to keep episcopal conferences in their place), not to mention more triumphant papal visits (most significantly to Cuba). A brief recounting of these events has been another element of the book's updating.

In this revised edition, no chapter has remained unchanged, and no chapter is entirely new. Chapters 1 through 5 are mostly written by Peter, but with seamless additions of new material. Chapter 6 and the extended look at candidates in Part Two are mostly written by me, but incorporate sections from Peter's original.

Chapter 6 begins with Peter's analysis of the nationalities of popes and goes on to question the common assumption that electing an Italian pope would be a retrograde step. The history of Hadrian VI, in the sixteenth century, shows that the current problems accompanying a Polish pope may be common to non-Italians in general.

The rundown in Part Two of every cardinal who will be in the conclave is the most substantial new section. It has been necessitated by the fact that the old short list is due for a radical rethinking as most of the obvious candidates reach their mid-seventies. The conclave could now be almost any-one's. Dare I say it, but this book would be a most useful reference manual for any cardinal to take into the conclave with him.

MARGARET HEBBLETHWAITE

September 19, 1999

PART I THE BACKGROUND

PRELUDE An Action of the Whole Church

The death of a pope is not an occasion for gloom. After all, a pope should be better prepared for death than most of us. When in 1958 Cardinal Angelo Roncalli heard the news of the death of Pope Pius XII, he wrote in his diary: "Sister death came swiftly and fulfilled her office. . . . One of my favorite phrases brings me great comfort: we are not on earth as museum-keepers, but to cultivate a flourishing garden of life and to prepare a glorious future. The Pope is dead, long live the Pope!"[1]

Nothing concentrates the mind of the Church so much as a conclave to elect a new pope. And nothing focuses the eyes of the world on Rome and the Vatican so much as a papal election in which the members of the college of cardinals, "the world's most exclusive club," awesomely choose the Successor of St. Peter, the Vicar of Christ on earth. ABC, CNN, CBC, CBS, NBC, Fox, and the world's other TV companies will have their cameras there—outside the walls. Commentators will be reduced to saying: "Behind those walls, history is being made."

The scene in the Sistine Chapel is familiar from movies like *The Cardinal* or the adaptation of Morris West's novel *The Shoes of the Fisherman*. But much of what they say or imply is out of date. This changeless institution has changed quite a lot. One medieval tradition will not be seen again. The seats where the cardinals sat around the Sistine Chapel were surmounted by canopies serving no known purpose except one. When a pope was elected, all the cardinals lowered their canopies, leaving only the new pope with his canopy up. Moreover, conclaves did not happen in the Sistine Chapel until after the collapse of the Papal States in 1870.

On the other hand, the method of voting has changed little over a millennium. The rules were devised to prevent cheating. On the tables are ballot papers with the printed formula *Eligo in Summum Pontificem* ("I elect as Supreme Pontiff"). Below, the cardinals write the name of their first-choice candidate—they are recommended to disguise their handwriting so no one can recognize it. This seems rather unnecessary, since the ballot papers are soon going to be burned—the puff of grayish black smoke they provide is the sign to the waiting world that a pope has not been elected. But the scrutineers might recognize the handwriting.

Then, having folded the paper twice, the cardinals advance one by one to the altar, holding the ballot in the air, and pronounce the oath: "I call as my witness Christ the Lord, who will be my judge that my vote is given to the one whom before God I think should be elected." The cardinal then places the ballot paper on the paten and tips it into the chalice on the altar. Then he bows to the altar and returns to his place. It is an awesome act beneath the gaze of

Michelangelo's severe, chastising Christ. It stands out in even more alarming and colorful fashion with the grime and candle smoke of centuries cleared away courtesy of the Nippon Television Network Corporation.

The election of a pope in a conclave is one of those institutions of the Catholic world that emerge from the abyss of time immemorial. Yet there is a great contrast between those of the first and second millenniums. After the Church emerged from the underground in the fourth century, the Bishop of Rome was elected by the parish priests of the city, and the man elected had to be accepted by the populace. In 1059 Pope Nicholas II restricted the electoral college to cardinals—at that date an unscriptural novelty of recent devising. But to this day each new cardinal is assigned a Rome church of which he is the nominal pastor. So the archbishop of Westminster in London has to "take possession" of the church of San Silvestro in downtown Rome before he can become a member of the college of cardinals.

There is another contrast between the conclaves of the Middle Ages and those of the last two centuries. In the late Middle Ages the college of cardinals was a tightly knit group of mostly Italians who deliberately wanted to keep their number small so as not to dilute their power. In 1517 Leo X (the Medici pope who said, "Now we have the papacy, let us at least enjoy it") executed one cardinal, imprisoned several others, and packed the college with thirty-one place-hunters. It was not the "cause" of the Reformation, but it helped. In 1586, the post-Tridentine Pope Sixtus V fixed the number of cardinals at not more than seventy. We had to wait until Pope John XXIII in 1958 for that rule to be breached.

After Vatican II (1962–65), the council summoned unexpectedly, indeed astonishingly, by Pope John XXIII, the idea of restricting the papal election to the college of cardinals seemed anomalous in a Church that now saw itself as the People of God on its pilgrim march through history. In the era of collegiality too many voices were excluded from the conclave—the voices of the local churches from four continents, of women, of the young or even the middle-aged, and above all of the poor; all are shut out. Paul VI wanted to change radically the arrangements for the conclave, made a brave start, and then drew back in alarm at what he had done.

He excluded the over-eighties—an incredibly controversial move, for the over-eighties at least. On Italian TV Cardinal Eugène Tisserant fumed, while Cardinal Alfredo Ottaviani's jowls wobbled with indignation. What Paul VI in effect did was to declare that being a cardinal did not carry with it a prescriptive *right* to elect the pope. It was a small change. But a small change is as important in principle as a big one: a future pope could realize Paul VI's original plan and, say, make the presidents of episcopal colleges the electoral college, whether they were cardinals or not.

Though this has not yet happened, something of the collegial mode of thinking inspired by Vatican II remains. Sometime in the third millennium one must expect the rules to be changed to reflect this. "It takes fifty to a hundred years for councils to have their effect," is the common judgment of Church historians. In any case, Paul VI envisaged the whole Church as somehow engaged or participating in a conclave—if only by prayer. He pictured the scene in the Acts of the Apostles where Mary, the mother of Jesus, is present among the disciples, and "the whole gathering/church persevered in prayer with one heart" (Acts 1:14). He goes on: "Thus the election of the new pope will not be an event isolated from the People of God which concerns only the electoral college, but, in a certain sense, it will be an action of the whole Church" (*Romano Pontifici Eligendo,* no. 85).

It is surely difficult to perceive the link between the gathering of terrified disciples in the upper room with Mary and indeed many other women in their midst and a papal conclave, just as it is hard to grasp the link between the Last Supper and Pontifical High Mass with clouds of billowing incense. Yet that is what Catholics have to do: discover their Christian and biblical origins.

Very instructive for conclave history is a book that appeared in 1877, while Pio Nono (as Pius IX was always known in the English-speaking world) was still reigning. When Ruggiero Bonghi published his *Pio Nono e il Papa futuro (Pius IX and the Future Pope)*, he was of course unaware that he was writing just one year before the death of Pio Nono. It was already the longest papacy in history, having lasted thirty-one years at that date. Perhaps that gives us a subsidiary law: don't appoint a young pope, or he will be around forever. Pio Nono was forty-six when elected; John Paul II was fifty-eight. Conventional wisdom said they were both much too young.

Back, however, to Bonghi in 1877. With unerring precision he correctly predicted that the next pope would be the archbishop of Perugia, Cardinal Gioachinno Pecci. How did he justify this? Quite simply by the fact that Pecci represented an *alternative* to Pio Nono in every respect.

Cardinal Pecci had stood aloof from the pontificate for the most part. He had set up an alternative court in Perugia, patronized learning and the arts, and written pastoral letters that had the sweep and scope of encyclicals for which they were dress rehearsals. No one else had done this so manifestly. No one else was a candidate. Of course, one can say that Bonghi's task was made easier by the length of Pio Nono's pontificate: the idea of an alternative, a radical change, was in the air, for by this time Pio Nono was unpopular in Italy.

Nothing new in that. All popes tend to grow in unpopularity toward the end of their reigns; and the longer they last, the more unpopular they become and the more they stand in the way of necessary change, becoming obstacles to responsiveness to the needs of the Church and the world. There is no Pecci around today, though Cardinal Carlo Maria Martini, the Jesuit from Milan, has some features in common with him.

There was in 1877 one obvious objection to Bonghi's theory of the need for an alternative pope: all the cardinals who would meet in the conclave to elect Pio Nono's successor had been "created"—the technical term—by the man himself; and it had to be presumed that they shared in his pessimistic, defensive view of the world. But—and this is another conclave law—however loyal cardinals may be to the pope who created them, they are not his creatures and they are in any case liberated by his death, freed to make a fresh start.

A statement describing the kind of pope needed for the new millennium was sent to all the cardinal electors on September 20, 1998, by the international reform group We Are Church. Beginning in Austria in 1995 as a result of the crisis provoked by the revelations of Cardinal Hans Hermann Groër's sexual abuse of young men, We Are Church spread around the world, though it nowhere else captured quite the enthusiasm it had in Austria, where its petition for reform gathered half a million signatures. Its statement "A Pope for the Time to Come: Bishop of Rome and Universal Pastor" is endorsed by groups in 146 countries, including 8 in Latin America, and 4 in Asia and South Africa. It is a long document, but the principal points are these:

We share our thought in the spirit of the woman in the Gospel who mixed yeast with flour so that her bread might expand and nourish a community. This is our "yeast."

A model of Church for our times: ever ancient, ever new . . .

To build a vibrant Church in the new millennium, we need to listen once again to Jesus and his first disciples who preached the equality of all persons. We need to build structures in our Church which reflect that equality. . . .

We need to restore a Church that values dialogue and justice in its internal life as well as its approach to the world. . . .

We begin by urging that we restore the practice of the early Church and develop structures that permit the People of God to participate in a prominent way in the election of all Church leaders. This would include the election of the Pope, the Bishop of Rome. . . .

We especially need a leader who recognizes the awakening of women's consciousness as a significant "sign of our times.". . .

We need a Pope who . . . would retire at the age established for all bishops. . . . He would reform the Curia so that it might serve, rather than dominate, other bishops and the Church universal.

But most of all, we need a Bishop of Rome and a Universal Pastor who is:

A visionary leader who promotes a profound discernment on Church ministry by all the People of God and calls them to consider the possibility of welcoming into ministry all those qualified, whatever their gender, marital status, or sexual orientation.

A respecter of the consciences of Catholics who calls forth a genuine public dialogue on the theologies, moral teaching, and policies in the Church . . .

A leader who recognizes the cultural pluralism of the Church and celebrates the diversity that flowers in different parts of our world . . .

An ecumenist who engages in serious dialogue . . .

A student of religious traditions other than Christianity and Judaism who welcomes interfaith dialogue . . .

A lover whose arms embrace the world and whose policies express a special solidarity with the poor and oppressed . . .

A lover of the earth who recognizes and promotes the integrity of all creation.

This vision is beyond any possibility at the moment, though the need for it will become more apparent when we consider what John Paul II has done to the legacy of the Second Vatican Council in Chapter 5. But it is perhaps a pointer to the future—not the future we are likely to get just yet, but the future that beckons us. It is not impossible that the cardinal electors will make some movement in this direction. Not probable, just not impossible.

Most cardinals know they are likely to experience only one conclave in their lives. They have enough sense of responsibility to wish to bring the voices of the young and the poor with them into the conclave. And they have enough conscience genuinely to ask themselves what the Spirit is saying to the churches today. If that law operated in 1878, after Bonghi had made his predictions, why should it not operate in 200x?

ONE The Next Conclave

Popes are elected for life, and there is no such thing as a deputy pope. Consequently no one is "a heartbeat away from the papacy." Yet someone has to take charge when the pope dies. In 1991 the Spanish Cardinal Eduardo Martínez Somalo was appointed *camerlengo,* or chamberlain. His first task will be to check that John Paul II is truly dead. This is traditionally done by tapping him on the forehead with a silver hammer.

Then he has to notify the cardinal vicar for Rome, Cardinal Camillo Ruini, who will tell the world. The *camerlengo* will then organize the funeral, to which world leaders will come. He will arrange for the *Novemdiales,* or nine days of mourning, and the lying in state of the body of the pope, attired in pontifical vestments, in the Vatican basilica. He will arrange for the destruction of the Fisherman's Ring and of the lead seal used for Apostolic Letters. He will place seals on the pope's study and bedroom. He will convene General Congregations during which the cardinals will praise the recently deceased pope, familiarize themselves with the rules for the coming election, and delicately hint at what sort of pope is needed next. But Martínez Somalo's main task is to organize the conclave itself. The one near certainty is that he will not be elected himself.

The assembly of cardinals that will elect Pope John Paul's successor is called a conclave because they are locked up *con clave* ("with a key"), preventing communication with the outside world. In previous conclaves they have actually been locked inside the Apostolic Palace, to the right of St. Peter's, which includes the Sistine Chapel, telephone wires were ripped out, and outward-looking windows were shuttered and sealed. But John Paul II has built the cardinals a new and comfortable hotel block, the Domus Sanctae Marthae (in Latin) or just the Santa Marta (in Italian)—St. Martha's— with 108 suites and 23 single rooms, all with private baths, but with rather thin walls so that conversations can be overheard. There are just enough rooms to accommodate the 120 cardinal electors plus the secretary of the college of cardinals, the master of papal liturgical celebrations, two masters of ceremonies, two religious attached to the papal sacristy, and an ecclesiastic to assist the cardinal dean. A couple of doctors and some cooks are also to be allowed inside, as well as some priests to hear confessions in the various languages spoken by the cardinals. All of these will take a solemn oath of secrecy.

From the Santa Marta the cardinals will be "transported" (presumably by bus) a mere stone's throw across the Vatican courtyards to the Apostolic Palace, under strict security so that no one can approach them along the way. Inside there will be no cameras, radios, televisions, tape recorders, mobile phones, modems, or fax machines. Two trustworthy technicians will search the buildings for bugging devices.

The cardinals will be totally incommunicado. They will be forbidden to make phone calls, send or receive messages, read newspapers, listen to the radio, or watch television.

Hundreds of journalists and television reporters will converge upon Rome, hoping in vain to break the security; instead, they will have to spin words and juggle speculations in the protracted news blackout. Much nonsense will be written. Bookmakers will offer odds. Fools will take them.

Yet a few things may be said with fair certainty about this future event. The conclave will be made up of a maximum of 120 cardinals none of whom will be over eighty (as of the day the previous pope died). Although the cardinals could theoretically elect any male Catholic, it is virtually certain that the next pope will be sitting there among them. So it is safe to assume that the next pope will be male and will emerge from the college of cardinals. According to the predictions customarily ascribed to the twelfth-century archbishop of Armagh, St. Malachy, his motto will be *Oliva pacis,* the "Olive branch of peace."

Beyond that, it is impossible to predict the result of the next conclave—for the simple reason that we do not know *when* it will occur. As of October 1999, John Paul II had already completed twenty-one years as pope. Undoubtedly we have entered the preconclave period that comes toward the end of any long pontificate.

This can be said without having any privileged insight into the state of Pope John Paul's health. For some years now, the Vatican has stopped denying that he is suffering from Parkinson's disease, a progressive degenerative condition that slows him down, makes him shake, and gives his face an impassive appearance. The shaking can be controlled by drugs, but the side effect is a slurring of the speech: John Paul is now very hard to understand when he speaks over a public address system, no matter what language he is using.

But Parkinson's is no quick killer. There have always been health scares, which Vatican watchers have seized on with alacrity. The first and most dramatic was in 1981 when a Turkish assassin, Mehmet Ali Agca, tried to kill him in St. Peter's Square on May 13, feast of Our Lady of Fátima. The two operations John Paul underwent for the removal of the bullets would have taxed the strength of a less tough constitution.

But he recovered, remarkably, attributing his escape to Our Lady of Fátima. On the first anniversary of the shooting, in 1982, he went to Fátima in Portugal and left behind one of the bullets as a memento. He was back again in 1991 on the tenth anniversary of the shooting. On his return to Rome he remarked, "I consider this entire decade to be a free gift, given to me in a special way by Divine Providence."[1] So he has had a sense of living on borrowed time and feels confirmed in his policies: if he has been spared by Divine Providence, it is surely for some purpose.

Eleven years after the failed assassination attempt, in July 1992, there was another health scare. John Paul underwent an operation for the removal of a tumor of the colon "about the size of an orange." It was reassuring to learn that it was a "benign growth," less so to realize that it had not been diagnosed earlier. But the Vatican press office would allow no word of criticism of the papal doctor, Dr. Renato Buzzonetti, and the press officer, Joaquín Navarro-Valls, insisted early in 1993 that the pope was fine:

> *I would say that he is more healthy than before. He has scars on his intestine which were removed along with the tumor. Now he is able to digest his food well. . . . The July 15 operation was definitive; there won't be another one. Three biopsies were done, before, during and after the operation. And there is something more: on January 18, 1993, the Holy Father underwent a complete checkup. All the tests gave results within the normal range.*

He pointed to the full and exhausting program of visits to Africa—including the politically delicate Sudan—to Albania, and in June to Spain as evidence of rude health.

Pope John Paul's state of health soon became the subject of Roman jokes—with the pope himself as the leading joker. After addressing the Food and Agriculture Organization of the United Nations on Sunday, November 14, 1993, he moved to his right, but an aide called him the other way and he missed a step, falling heavily on his right shoulder and dislocating it. He got up unaided, paused for a moment, and then continued to shake hands and bless with his left hand. There had been no blackout. A night in Rome's Gemelli Hospital put his right shoulder back in place.

The next time he appeared in public, Saturday, November 20, 1993, his right arm was hidden by a sling beneath his crimson cape so that, he quipped, "the photographers cannot immortalize this deficient pope and show him to the world." "But you have a right to see it, a right to see it," he went on, causing one optimistic commentator to enthuse that the pope was "thus paying tribute to the mass media." John Paul made a mistake in Italian (though some claimed he did it on purpose). He kept on using the word *deficiente* as though he thought it meant physically weak; in fact it means mentally disadvantaged. As soon as he sat down on his throne in the Nervi audience hall for the meeting with the health workers organized by Cardinal Fiorenzo Angelini, he declared: "As you can see, the pope is a bit *deficiente*—but he's not finished yet." Mild titters. "The deficient pope greets all of you," he plunged on, "but he's not yet in a state of collapse [*decaduto*]." More laughter.

Being a polyglot has its disadvantages. In Colombia, John Paul was asked what he most enjoyed eating during his stay there. "*El hombre* [man]," he cannibalistically replied, thinking the question was about what he had most enjoyed, period.

Marco Politi of *La Repubblica* contrived an interview with Professor Corrado Manni, chief anesthetist at Gemelli Hospital, which began to give a more serious view of John Paul's health. On the plane to Denver in August 1993, Politi noticed that John Paul's left hand was constantly trembling. He tried to disguise this by holding it steady with his right hand or, when seated, by leaning on his left hand with his head characteristically on one side. Now that his left hand had to do all the work, it was harder to conceal the trembling.

Politi asked Manni what the significance of this was. Manni replied: "There could be lots of causes. There could, for example, be neurological reasons. Or there could be a slight trembling in moments of special stress. But it cannot in any case be related to the tumor that has been cleared up. There could be many different causes. In another person—I stress in another person—Parkinson's disease could begin like that." Despite the cautious formulation, both Manni and Politi got into hot water with the Vatican press office for this remark.

Manni's explanation for the fact that John Paul often seems listless in the morning and then brightens up in the course of the day was that "he leads an infernal life, getting up at 5:30 in the morning, and working a seventeen-hour day." The pope is strong as an ox, said Manni, but with the years and the overwork he has imposed on himself, "there are bound to be signs of tiredness." In Manni's opinion the pope should try to lead a quieter life. He had once said, "Holy Father, couldn't you work a little less?" To which the pope replied with astonishment, "You mean, *still less?*" In his own mind he has already made enough concessions to his medical advisers.

But then, just three weeks before his seventy-fourth birth-day (May 18, 1994), he slipped and fell getting out of his bath at 11:00 P.M. on Thursday, April 28. Dr. Renato Buzzonetti was soon on the scene. An X-ray examination revealed that John Paul had broken his right femur (thigh bone). A mild sedative enabled him to sleep through the night; it was thought he would be better prepared for surgery if he were properly rested. Next morning at 10:00 A.M. he was taken to the Gemelli Hospital. He was getting to know the place well: this was his sixth stay there. The official medical bulletin, signed by four physicians, said simply: "Tests given at the hospital con-firmed the earlier diagnosis of a fracture of the right femur. The pope then underwent surgery for arthro-prosthesis. The operation lasted about two hours." It was all very formal. Gianfranco Fineschi, who performed the surgery, attempted a joke: "From now on the pope will not have the hip that God made, but one a bioengineer made."

Back in the Vatican press office, Joaquín Navarro-Valls, whose medical qualifications ensure a good command of technical vocabulary, insisted that the pope's general health remained good. He "absolutely excluded the possibility of the pope losing consciousness or feeling sick, either before or after the fall." In other words, the fall was an accident such as might happen to anyone in bare feet on those slip-pery Roman marble floors. But this time there were graver consequences. The pope would never ski again, never climb another mountain, and have pain even when he walked.

In Zagreb, capital of Croatia, in September 1994, John Paul was unable to prostrate himself to kiss the ground, so the turf of Zagreb was raised to his lips on an elegant dish. True, having been raised to the altar by an invisible eleva-tor, John Paul abandoned his two canes and greeted the million-strong crowd with expansive gestures north, south, east, and west. But that proved he responded to crowds, not that he was better. In late September his face began to acquire its now familiar but disconcerting look, with his right eye hanging permanently puffy and open and the left eye closed to a slit.

Since then the decline has been constant and plain for all to see, though those who speak with him have always stressed that his sluggish appearance is misleading: he retains an astonishing mental alertness, though he may be slow in communicating this. The media hawks are on alert every time he misses an engagement. At Christmas 1995, he had to interrupt his *Urbi et Orbi* ("To the city and the world") blessing because of a bout of nausea. In March 1996, he cancelled an audience because of a digestive problem, and a similar recurrence made him miss a Mass at Castel Gandolfo in August the same year. It was back to hospital again in October, to be operated on for appendicitis. That year was the first for which no Christmas morning Mass was scheduled for him. In February 1997 he cancelled an audience because of flu, and in November the same year missed a Mass because he had a temperature. In December 1998, he suspended his audiences because of a fever. Another spot of temperature made him cancel an audience with the mayor of Rome in February 1999. Saddest for him was the flu that made him cancel Mass in his old diocese of Kraków during his June 1999 visit to Poland. But these few scattered days of illness compare favorably with the sick days of almost any employee.

Still, the pope is not immortal, and a preconclave atmosphere has begun to be felt increasingly, even within the Vatican itself. Leo XIII, who just made it into this century, died in 1903 at the age of ninety-three. His lengthy reign led a cardinal to remark: "We elected a Holy Father, not an eternal father." Such longevity in popes cannot be taken for granted. Only 9 out of the last 246 popes have lasted more than twenty years. In the twentieth century, no pope has been longer on the throne of Peter than John Paul II. The nearest rival is Pius XII, who clocked up nineteen years; John Paul has already passed his twenty-first anniversary in the job.

It is anathema in Rome to talk openly about the end of the pontificate. It is thought to undermine the policies of the present pontiff by stirring up hope for a new line and suggesting there is lame-duck leadership. Equally shunned are discussions about possible resignation, for which there are not many precedents. Four popes abdicated: Clement I, number three after Peter, in 97; Pontian, in 235, to allow a successor to take over when he was carted off to Sardinia and the mines; Benedict IX, in 1045 (though he made a comeback); and Celestine V, in 1294, the last pope to resign.[2] All except Benedict were canonized.

Paul VI went to visit St. Celestine's tomb at Anagni in 1966. Everyone thought—wrongly, as it turned out—that he was hinting at his own imminent resignation when he said, "After a few months St. Celestine understood that he was being deceived by those who surrounded him." John Paul does not have that reason for resigning. Nor need he expect to be unseated, or deposed, as were seven of his predecessors between 537 and 1048.

But there is a new factor since Vatican II. The Church is less of a gerontocracy than it was as recently as the 1950s, due to two reforms introduced by Paul VI. The retirement age for cardinals is eighty, and the over-eighties cannot take part in the conclave. Bishops must tender their resignation to the pope when they reach seventy-five, though it is not always accepted. In theory it would not be unreasonable to imagine a Bishop of Rome retiring at eighty—if the over-eighties are incapable of electing a pope, how can one of their number do the job?—or resigning at seventy-five.

Jean Chélini, a French historian close to the late Cardinal Jacques Martin, hinted as long ago as 1984 that Pope John Paul had considered a certain "scenario of resignation." He concludes his book *Au Vatican de Jean-Paul II* thus:

> *Certain intimates of Pope John Paul II give one to understand that he will retire at seventy-five and, after a "sportive" sabbatical year, would retire to the Carmelite convent he wanted to enter as a young student. Is it this prospect that makes John Paul so serene, so cheerful, like a man who is certain about the future?*

But John Paul reached the age of seventy-five on May 18, 1995, and showed himself no quitter.

There is a rumor that he has signed a secret letter of resignation that could be activated if he became senile—a prudent precaution that could save the Church from a very embarrassing situation, though for the usual reasons no one will confirm that such a document exists. Apart from the eventuality of total incapacity to do the job, Vatican watchers are no longer anticipating a resignation.

Yet the preconclave mood intensifies the longer the pontificate grinds on. Nor can one say that speculation about the succession is confined to "irresponsible journalists." It is the stuff of private conversations in the Curia, whose members read the works of the "irresponsible journalists" with knowing winks and dismissive shrugs.

Here is an example from my own experience. In an article published originally in the *Irish Times* and the *National Catholic Reporter* back in September 1992, I offered a classic list of three names (a *terna*). I stressed that these were not predictions, said that everything depended on the timing, and confessed that I had not the faintest idea who would be the next pope. But if there were a conclave fairly soon, I carefully explained, these were the names that sprang to mind.

I began with Cardinal Carlo Maria Martini, archbishop of Milan, as the best equipped, intellectually and spiritually, to succeed. Objection: he is a Jesuit, and not only has there never been a Jesuit pope, there has never before been a Jesuit cardinal who was a serious candidate for the papacy. Next came Cardinal Pio Laghi, former nuncio in Argentina and the United States, who was said by good sources to be "the candidate of the U.S. cardinals." Objection: he is intellectually lightweight and (born May 22, 1922) only two years younger than Pope John Paul. His chances decrease the longer the pontificate goes on.

But it was my third, the long shot, the dark horse, that aroused most interest. For a Third World candidate I proposed Nigerian Cardinal Francis J. Arinze, president since 1984 of the Pontifical Council for Inter-religious Dialogue. As such, he has been responsible for dialogue with Muslims, who form half the population of Nigeria. He has had very good relations with them. He has shown himself capable of running a Roman office—though a small one—and proved a good talent spotter, an essential attribute for a pope.

If the great achievement of John Paul II is to have "dealt with" Communism, then undoubtedly the next challenging task for the papacy will be dealing with Islam. For that Cardinal Arinze is better equipped than anyone else. And he is black: that would strike the imagination of the world, just as the "Polishness" of Karol Wojtyla captured it in 1978.

The point of this story is what happened next. Two months later I met the secretary of the Pontifical Council for Interreligious Dialogue, Bishop Michael Fitzgerald. He looked very severe and said I had behaved very badly and irresponsibly, causing "great difficulties" to his cardinal, who was "very displeased." I inquired what those difficulties were. After all, though calumny and detraction are to be avoided, it is not injurious to someone's reputation to suggest he could conceivably be elected pope. But that was not the point. Apparently, some people were too scared to issue invitations to Cardinal Arinze henceforth, on the grounds that they might seem to be "currying favor" with the "next pope." An awkwardness was introduced into relationships.

Of course what had happened was that my highly tentative, nuanced remarks had become virtual certainties by the time they reached Nigeria. Prestigious newspapers in Europe and America carried headlines stating "NIGERIAN NEXT POPE." The Muslim papers took it up enthusiastically, especially of course in Nigeria. This cautionary tale has another lesson. Although Cardinal Arinze was "displeased," he began tut-tutting only after he had time to think about it and adjust his attitudes—his immediate reaction had been one of pleasure that someone had thought of him. "Ibos are never lacking in self-confidence," said the source.

This book is not only about who may become the next pope. That is only the half of it. A conclave throws the spotlight on the Vatican in a way nothing else does. For a few weeks the cardinals of the college are scrutinized with great intensity. Nothing is so much fun as an unpredictable election. But it is also an opportunity to ask where the Church stands. It raises the fundamental question, as articulated by the Italian *vaticanista* Giancarlo Zizola: "What sort of pope do we need in what sort of Church for what sort of world?"[4]

Of course it is the college of cardinals, and the college of cardinals alone, who actually have to decide whom to elect on the basis of these discussions. But they are not, and would not wish to be, sundered from the rest of the Church. They carry the whole Church with them in their deliberations.

Nor can it be said that speculation about the succession is confined to "irresponsible journalists." Cardinal Achille Silvestrini, prefect of the Congregation for the

Oriental Churches, born October 25, 1923, will be present at any conclave occurring before 2003. He is the first cardinal publicly to share his thoughts on the subject—without of course giving any names. He could be a key figure.

In an interview published in the Italian geopolitical review *Limes*, Cardinal Silvestrini recalled that all popes in the nineteenth century came from the Papal States, over which, up till 1870, they were the temporal as well as the spiritual rulers. In the twentieth century, the circle widened to include anyone born in Italy. Three were patriarchs of Venice: St. Pius X, John XXIII, and John Paul I. Two were archbishops of Milan: Pius XI and Paul VI. Benedict XV came from Bologna and Pius XII, the only Roman-born pope of the century, was in the Curia as cardinal secretary of state under his predecessor, Pius XI.

Cardinal Silvestrini maintained that with the election of a Polish pope, John Paul II, in October 1978, the geographical boundaries have been overcome and "anything becomes possible." The next pope would be chosen, he suggested, not on grounds of nationality, but on grounds of personality: "In the future, who knows? It could well be that a Latin American or an African would emerge."[5] This corresponds to a widespread feeling that "no one is foreigner in Rome." The universal Church is not bedeviled by narrow nationalism. Because John Paul II broke through the nationality barrier, the next conclave will be the most open ever.

However, Cardinal Silvestrini's remarks may be considered obvious: their main interest is that they show a cardinal who is actively thinking about the next conclave. If *his* thoughts run along these lines, then other cardinals may well have similar thoughts—but they keep them to themselves.

But Cardinal Silvestrini's remarks neglect to mention a vital element. Whom are the cardinals electing? It may seem obvious to say that they are electing "a pope." But in the early Church (and still in the Orthodox churches) *pope* merely means "father," and it was applied to all priests. The Copts of Egypt call their patriarch "pope." In any case *pope* has no theological content, and the term is never used in conciliar documents. Vatican Council I speaks, grandly, of the Roman pontiff, or *Pontifex Romanus* ("the Roman bridge-builder")—a title that harks back to the Roman emperors.

But the fundamental title for the pope is Bishop of Rome, the successor of St. Peter, and this is the foundation of all the grander titles: Primate of Italy, Patriarch of the West, Pontiff of the Universal Church. Rome needs a bishop. The next pope should therefore be, if not an Italian, then at least an Italian speaker. A pope who could not address the crowd in St. Peter's Square in their own language is almost inconceivable. If true, that narrows the field—though perhaps not by very much. It would exclude most North American cardinals for a start.

The cardinals, nominally the parish priests of Rome, are electing their bishop, and not merely in a nominal sense. Pius XII (1939–58) had such an exalted view of "sacred Rome" (the *sacra città*) that he was unable to pay much attention to his diocese. He sacralized Rome to make it the heart and center of the universal Church of which he was the universal pastor. He rarely emerged from the Vatican (except to console the victims of the air raid on San Lorenzo in July 1943). Roman-born though he was, he seemed to regard the diocese as little more than his point of insertion into the wider world.

Pope John XXIII (1958–63) had a different view. He made a point of *acting* as the bishop of Rome because Rome needed a bishop. He regarded Rome, said the Italian Church historian Giuseppe Alberigo, "as his own church, the one for whose salvation he was responsible, the first guarantee of everything else he did."[6] Pope John was not just a theoretical bishop of Rome: he visited its prisons, hospitals, and above all parishes. He made much of his "taking possession" of St. John Lateran, his true cathedral (the basilica of St. Peter's belongs to the whole Church), and thought of moving his office there.

So the cardinals are electing, in the first place, a bishop of Rome. That has consequences, as a glance at history will show.

TWO Learning from the Past

In the first millennium, popes did not emerge from the college of cardinals, since cardinals in the modern sense did not yet exist. "By the beginning of the twelfth century," writes John F. Brodrick, S.J., in his historical study of cardinals in *Archivum Historiae Pontificiae*, "the entire sacred college acted as the elective body for the selection of Roman Pontiffs. Official recognition of this practice came in 1179 at Lateran Council III in the decree *Licet de evitanda*. Ever since then the college has retained this enormous power."[1]

If we take 1179 as the conservative starting point for the history of conclaves, that gives us ninety-four conclaves to analyze. The medieval and Renaissance ones cannot be dealt with here. The last two hundred years will provide enough material for reflection and instruction. The first rule is that all conclaves are the same and yet each one is different. Certain patterns recur; some lessons—one cannot call them laws—emerge. But nearly every time there is a new factor.

In the early nineteenth century, the "Catholic powers" of Europe took a great interest in who was pope, since the pope was also a temporal sovereign, the ruler of the Papal States. They ordered their ambassadors to veto (the right of "exclusion") unsound candidates and intrigue for their own favorites. A conclave was a highly political event. François-René de Chateaubriand, the man whose book *Le Génie du Christianisme* made religion fashionable again after the French Revolution, intrigued for France. He wanted a liberal pope.[2] All this off-stage activity meant that rigorous secrecy was impossible to maintain.

Antonio Rosmini, founder of the Rosminians and author of *The Five Wounds of the Church*, reported the latest gossip to the bishop of Trent, which was then part of Austria:

> The conclave is this time being held at the Quirinal. The Cardinals left the church of San Silvestro on foot and the Veni Creator was sung among an immense concourse of people. . . . Three more cardinals went in yesterday [making forty in all]. Our cardinals are there, that is the Hungarian and one from Milan, but not the Archduke Rudolph and the French Cardinals. I do not think the Spanish and Portuguese will come, partly because they are too old and partly because they are too busy.
>
> In the first scrutinies it is stated as a fact that Cardinal Pacca had twenty votes: he only needed five more for two-thirds.
>
> M. de Chateaubriand said he wanted Cardinal Pacca excluded, but this appears to have been a private bombshell for he had not yet received his credentials from the court to the Sacred College. Nothing is known of the scrutinies that followed, but it seems that Pacca is out of the running. This cardinal has the reputation of great piety, of being a good theologian and a

good administrator, but he is supposed to be too gentle and easy to influence. He gained a great reputation during the persecution of Pius VII. As Pacca's supporters have not succeeded, it is thought that the Conclave will be somewhat prolonged.[3]

Rosmini was right about that. The conclave ran from February 23 to March 31, 1829, being further delayed by the late arrival of Cardinal Giuseppe Albani, who held the "veto" of the Austrian emperor. The veto, in effect the right to blackball certain candidates, meant that the conclave was not "free." However, stretching a point, it could be said to represent the last vestige of "lay involvement" in the process of choosing a pope.

The result was that a compromise candidate, Cardinal Francesco Saverio Castiglioni, was elected and took the name Pius VIII. But he was sixty-eight and in such bad health that he was unable to celebrate the liturgy in public. He lasted only twenty months, dying in 1830 as revolution broke out in France, Poland and Hungary, and the Papal States.

MORAL: Don't elect a sick pope.

The 1830 conclave was conditioned by this political situation. The Austrian statesman Klemens von Metternich wanted a strong pope who would not "give way to the madness of the age." He found his man in Bartolomeo Alberto Cappellari, author in 1799 of a courageous, *un*–politically correct book called *The Triumph of the Holy See and the Church Against the Attacks of Innovators.* A Camaldolese monk (a very strict contemplative), he took the name Gregory XVI partly in memory of his twenty years as abbot of San Gregorio on the Coelian Hill. From this abbey Gregory the Great dispatched Augustine to Canterbury and England in 596. Gregory XVI had a more immediate link with England in that he knew the Italian Passionist Dominic Barberi, who received John Henry Newman into the Church in 1845, and Nicholas Wiseman, who in 1850 became the first archbishop of Westminster.

But the conclave lasted fifty days and was very onerous. This time the Spanish veto worked against Cardinal Giustiniani, who was related to the English Catholic aristocracy via the Clifford and the Weld families. As in 1829, Cardinal Albani led the intrigues: an intercepted note showed him to be working against Cappellari, and his candidate, Macchi, stalled at twelve votes. Cappellari became pope. He gave Albani and Metternich every satisfaction on the ideological front.

MORAL: Don't elect a pope on the basis of his writings, and don't elect a theologian—he will be unable to leave theology to others.

Thus we reach June 1846, when Pius IX, invariably known, thanks to Mr. Gladstone, as Pio Nono, began the longest pontificate history has ever known—nearly thirty-two years. (John Paul notched up twenty-one, before the dawn of the new millennium.) It brought to an end the series of conclaves held in the centuries-old lifetime of the Papal States. For the last time, the fifty out of sixty-two cardinals who came to Rome (twelve did not make it in time) were electing not just the bishop of Rome, but the temporal sovereign of the Papal States. The Papal States, already embryonically present when Gregory the Great sent St. Augustine to England in 596, by the nineteenth century boasted a police force and a judiciary that imprisoned or executed "liberals." It was also the last conclave to be held in the Quirinal, the pope's Roman summer residence until the collapse of the Papal States in 1870. (Since then it has been the official residence of the president of Italy.)

It proved a bruising contest. The leading candidates were Cardinal Luigi Lambruschini, who wanted to continue the highly conservative policies of Gregory XVI, who notoriously banned railroads on the grounds that *chemins de fer* ("railways") were *chemins d'enfer* ("ways to hell"). His chief opponent, Giovanni Maria Mastai Ferretti, bishop of Imola, blithely brought along the latest pamphlets depicting papal primacy as the hope of liberal Italy. His intention was to present them to the new pope.

On June 14, 1846, those cardinals capable of walking processed from the church of San Silvestro (now the titular church of cardinal archbishops of Westminster) to the Quirinal. Mastai Ferretti may not have expected to become pope, but behind the scenes two important cardinals were working on his behalf. The Roman Cardinal Polidori joined forces with Cardinal Micara to organize the defeat of Lambruschini. Here we see the concept of the *grande elettore*, a "kingmaker" or "popemaker," who intrigues on behalf of others, but is not himself a candidate.

The 1846 election also dramatized the issue of continuity versus change, which, with many variants, is always at issue in a conclave. Mastai Ferretti's supporters wanted a different sort of papacy, one that would take the lead in uniting Italy and "modernizing" the Papal States; Lambruschini, as the dauphin of Gregory XVI, wanted to continue his counterrevolutionary policies.

In the first ballot of June 15, Lambruschini had fifteen votes to Mastai Ferretti's thirteen; by the second ballot Mastai Ferretti was ahead seventeen to thirteen. The next day Mastai Ferretti led twenty-seven to eleven in the third ballot and clinched it thirty-six to ten in the fourth. However, this victory in the fourth ballot was secured by a device called *accessus*, now strictly banned: when the result of a ballot was announced and before proceeding to the next vote, a cardinal could announce that he was annulling his previous vote and rallying to the majority. The cardinal scrutineers *(recognitores)* made the switch. On this occasion in

1846 nine cardinals exercised the option. The maneuver, of course, meant that for those who changed their minds *the ballot was not secret;* so they could be—and were—accused of currying favor or seeking influence with the pope they helped to elect. That is why this custom was abolished.

As Pius IX, Mastai Ferretti was the last pope of the *ancien régime* in every sense of the term. He ruled over a court in which the favor of and patronage of the prince were all-decisive for the careers of his courtiers. His short-lived "liberalism" was largely confined to matters such as railways and gas lighting. "We had reckoned on everything," said Metternich, "except a liberal pope." He did not have long to worry about that. Soon the liberal pope was fleeing revolution in Rome to Gaeta in 1849, disguised as a woman.

MORAL: The cardinals do not always get what they bargain for—they elect a man on one set of assumptions, only to find he does something completely different.

That same year the Polish romantic poet Juliusz Slowacki, exiled in Paris, wrote a poem in which he forecast that the twentieth century would see a Slavic pope:

> *This pope will not—Italian-like—take fright*
> *At cannon's roar or sabre-thrust*
> *But brave as God himself stand and give fight—*
> *His world—but dust . . .*
> *Love he dispenses as great powers today*
> *Distribute arms:*
> *With sacramental power—his sole array—*
> *The world he charms.*

As a boy in Katowice and Kraków, Karol Wojtyla, the future Pope John Paul II, knew Slowacki's poem by heart.

Pius IX was coldly received by the Roman populace in 1846 when he showed himself to them on June 17—partly because rumor based on the size of habits ordered by the papal tailor suggested a more popular and different-shaped candidate, Cardinal Gizzi. So sure were Gizzi's servants that his election was in the bag that they had already rashly burned his cardinal's robes.

If rumor has largely ceased to be a factor in papal elections, the first appearance of a new pope before the Roman people remains an important test, for it is a last faint flicker of the participation of the people of Rome in the election of their bishop. His "reception" by the Roman People of God still counts.

Both John Paul I and John Paul II were warmly received by the Roman people. The former, Albino Luciani, patriarch of Venice, won them by his charm and choice of double-barreled name. Having neither the wisdom of heart of Pope John XXIII nor the vast experience of Paul VI, he appealed to both of them. On his death, posters went up anticipating and welcoming "Pope John Paul II." Cardinal Karol Wojtyla accepted this name, though he might have preferred "Stanislaus." He won the Romans by his lilting Italian and by the fact that he was Polish. He captured their hearts when we went out on the balcony on the night of October 16, 1978, and said he would speak to them in "your language—no, our Italian language."

When Leo XIII was elected in 1878, he was not able to "show himself" to the Roman populace. With the collapse of the Papal States in 1870, the pope had become the self-styled "prisoner of the Vatican." Thus immured, he was unable to go about his diocese of Rome and left it in the charge of his vicar. Pius IX had been extremely unpopular, especially in anticlerical circles. Cries of "Throw the old dolt into the river" were heard as his body was being transferred to its final resting place.

The election of Gioacchino Pecci as Leo XIII came as a relief after the thirty-two years of Pio Nono, but it was not a surprise. Bonghi's book (see Prelude) had prepared minds for Leo's election.

MORAL: Cardinals, even when created by the pope just deceased and on the whole admiring him, do not necessarily vote for someone in the same mold.

Pius IX had rejected modernity, but Leo XIII sought prudently to embrace it. Although restricted in what he could do in Italy—he remained the "prisoner of the Vatican"—he patched up the quarrel with Germany after the disastrous *Kulturkampf,* sought the friendship of England, made peace with Switzerland, did his best to rally nostalgic French Catholics to their republic, tried to be on good terms with the czar of Russia, and even wrote to the emperor of China inviting him to protect missionaries.

One of Leo's first acts was to make John Henry Newman, the most celebrated convert of the nineteenth century, a cardinal. He revived the study of the philosophy and theology of St. Thomas Aquinas *(Aeterni Patris).* He opened the Vatican Library to scholars, declaring that "the Church has nothing to fear from the truth." Most important of all, with *Rerum Novarum* in 1891, he inaugurated the Church's "social teaching" denouncing impartially unbridled collectivism and unbridled individualism (or liberalism). This set the pattern for subsequent pontiffs to follow. The anniversary of *Rerum Novarum* was marked by *Quadragesimo Anno* in 1931, *Octogesimo Anno* in 1971, and John Paul II's *Centesimus Annus* in 1991. Never before had an encyclical letter been so influential and positive. It showed that the loss of the Papal States had liberated the papacy for a more spiritual role on the international scene.

Leo XIII was sixty-seven when elected in 1878. Conventional conclave wisdom said (and still says) that is about the right age, leading to an active pontificate of about ten years. But Leo XIII went on and on, celebrating his twenty-fifth anniversary as pope in 1903 when he was an astonishing ninety-three. As often happens, the cardinal electors of 1878 may have gotten what they wanted, but they also got more than they bargained for.

This made the conclave of 1903, at the dawn of the twentieth century, particularly fraught with tension. With sixty-three cardinal electors, the successful candidate had to reach two-thirds, or forty-two. The candidate most suited to continue the open-minded policies of Leo XIII was Mariano Rampolla, his secretary of state, the man effectively in charge as Leo aged. Rampolla was in the lead for the first two days, gaining twenty-four votes in the first ballot, twenty-nine in the second and third, and reaching thirty in the fourth. Then he stalled. His main opponent, Cardinal Giuseppe Gotti, had a mere seventeen.

The usual explanation for Rampolla's failure is that the cardinal archbishop of Kraków, Kniaz de Kolzielsko Puzyna, exercised the "veto" on behalf of the Austrian emperor, Franz-Joseph. That would mean that the conclave secret had been breached. Certainly this was the twentieth-century conclave most conditioned by political considerations on the part of the leading "Catholic" power of the day (republican and anticlerical France having forfeited this role). But it was not the only factor. An intransigent opposition of five cardinals was determined to stop Rampolla. In the first ballot they voted for Giuseppe Sarto, patriarch of Venice. Their votes and those that had gone to Gotti made up the one-third needed to block Rampolla. Manifestly he could not win, and his votes declined from the fifth ballot to twenty-four, then to thirteen and ten. Sarto played the card of humility: after the fourth ballot he declared "I will renounce the cardinalate and become a Capuchin friar." It seemed to work, for he had thirty-five votes in the sixth ballot, and in the seventh he became pope.

MORAL: Mistrust false humility and simple-minded piety masquerading as pastoral policy.

Sarto made his intentions clear by taking the name Pius. The pontificate of Leo XIII had been an interlude between the two Piuses. At first the comparison with his predecessor worked to his advantage. Pius X was simpler and more homely. Leo had received Catholics, with the exception of cardinals, kings, and princes, on their knees, but Pius sat them all down and chatted amiably. No one could have imagined the regally imperious Leo teaching catechism to children or swapping jokes with his coachman. Pius X gave the impression of being an unworldly, unpolitical, spiritual pope, the whole world's parish priest.

It was a faulty impression. Pius X, a simple-minded man, was obsessed with orthodoxy. This comes through even in the historical study (known as the *Disquisitio*) designed to promote his beatification. He saw perils everywhere. His 1907 encyclical *Pascendi Domenici Gregis* first invented "Modernism" as a pernicious theological system and then condemned it with great vigor. It included a disciplinary section that meant commissions of inquiry in all dioceses of Italy (at least) and wholesale oustings of seminary professors. Pius X encouraged purges, witch-hunts, and denunciations. The efficient espionage system, organized by Monsignor Umberto Benigni, was exposed thanks to the accidental discovery of a cache of documents in Ghent during World War I. The *Disquisitio* pretends that Pius X had nothing directly to do with these events and blames overzealous subordinates.

Pius X died on August 20, 1914, his heart broken, said his hagiographers, by the outbreak of a war he had warned against, but been unable to prevent. After the shambles of the 1903 conclave, Pius X imposed even stricter secrecy rules. This did not prevent the Austrian foreign minister, Count Berchtold, from instructing his ambassador to the

Holy See: "Cardinal Ferrata is considered Francophile and Cardinal Maffi is too much of an Italian nationalist, while the Benedictine Serafini seems the most pious, learned and free from political prejudices." Serafini, in short, would be the least troublesome candidate for the Central Powers.

But the plan or plot did not work. The mood of the conclave was somber, with cardinals from all the belligerents present. The French Jesuit Louis Billot had already lost a nephew on the front. Fifty-seven cardinals went into the conclave, eight being absent for reasons of ill health. The four ballots on September 1 showed Giacomo della Chiesa, archbishop of Bologna, neck and neck with Maffi, but gradually nosing ahead: twelve to twelve, sixteen to sixteen, eighteen to sixteen, twenty-one to fifteen.

That evening the cardinal archbishop of Cologne, Hartmann, sensing the danger, remarked that "to elect della Chiesa would be an affront to the memory of Pius X, since he had been undersecretary of state under Rampolla in the time of Leo XIII, and had continued to work in the spirit of Leo, thus causing his removal to Bologna."[4] Della Chiesa was described as "mediocre," no more than a good bureaucrat, and characterized by a "violent temper."

The slanderous discrediting of candidates has been a feature of conclaves. It is rarely effective, and sometimes boomerangs. In 1914 it failed altogether. The majority of cardinals thought being different from Pius X and reviving the spirit of Leo XIII a positive advantage as Europe plunged headlong into the most devastating war it had hitherto known. With Maffi dropped, the Benedictine Serafini became leader of the opposition. On September 2, della Chiesa gradually consolidated his lead: twenty to ten, twenty-seven to seventeen, thirty-one to twenty-one, and thirty-two to twenty-one. But he still needed six more votes, which he just achieved on September 3, winning thirty-eight to eighteen.

Of the three American cardinals, only Cardinal John J. Farley, archbishop of New York, described as "liberal for an American," actually managed to vote. He had prudently positioned himself in Switzerland. At this time cardinals had ten days to get to Rome. William H. O'Connell of Boston and the eighty-year-old James Gibbons of Baltimore did their best to beat the deadline, with O'Connell hiring a limousine in Naples. But it made no difference. They arrived together in Rome to the sound of bells and rejoicing at the election of della Chiesa.[5]

MORAL: Cardinals should never say, or think, that they cannot elect X or Y because to do so would constitute "an insult to the memory of his predecessor still warm in his grave."

The new pope made his intentions clear in his choice of name: Benedict XV. Benedict had been the name of the fictional pope in Antonio Fogazzaro's novel *Il Santo*, which Pius X had ludicrously put on the Index of Forbidden Books. As far as possible he would be a pope of peace, which led him in 1917 to declare the war "a useless slaughter" *(inutile strage),* a phrase that united all the belligerents against him. It was repeated by Pope John Paul II during the Gulf War of 1991.

But the clearest sign of Benedict's repudiation of the policies of his predecessor came in his first encyclical letter, *Ad Beatissimi Apostolorum* of November 1, 1914. It put an end to the habit of witch-hunting and denunciations, which appeared blasphemously irrelevant as Europe plunged into a fratricidal civil war. "There is no need to add epithets to the profession of Catholicism," said Benedict. "It is enough for each to say, *Christianus mihi nomen, Catholicus cognomen* [Christian is my name, and Catholic is my family name]. What matters is to live up to these names in one's life."

Since candidates for the papacy are not allowed to present an electoral platform, their first encyclical is often a programmatic statement, a declaration of intent. Benedict's misfortune was to be elected pope at a time when Europe was deafened by heavy artillery fire. He deserves rehabilitation. He emptied the Vatican coffers to provide humanitarian aid to Soviet Russia. He enabled Italian Catholics to return to political life by agreeing to the foundation of the Partito Popolare Italiano. Under its first secretary (that is, leader), the fiery and profound Sicilian priest Don Luigi Sturzo, it was the main challenger to the rise of Fascism. He reorganized Catholic missions, shifting their headquarters from Paris to Rome. He was urged to write an encyclical on "nationalism" as the greatest scourge and heresy of the twentieth century. Though willing enough, he ran out of time, dying within five days of flu that unexpectedly turned into pneumonia. He was "only" sixty-seven. There was much that his successor could build upon.

Benedict died on January 17, 1922. Giovanni Battista Montini (the future Pope Paul VI), then twenty-five, snuffling with his annual bout of flu, sketched out a portrait of "the sort of pope" the Church needed:

> The Church is about to be embodied in a man who after twenty centuries should represent not only the powerful Christ, but the Christ who is evangelical, peace-loving, holy and poor. Let us pray that we may merit a pope who is very like Jesus; and for that he will have to be crucified by the world that hates what it not its own; its salvation demands as much.[6]

This picture may have fitted John XXIII in 1958, whom the young Montini would meet in 1925, two years after he wrote these words. But this evangelical and "utopian" vision of the papacy was hardly fulfilled by Achille Ratti, emerging on February 6, 1922, after the bloodiest conclave of the twentieth century.

Two cardinals, at least, were excommunicated for breaking the rules. According to the *Memoirs* of Cardinal Pietro Gasparri, which languish unpublished in the Vatican archives, they were La Fontaine, patriarch of Venice, and the Anglophile Rafael Merry del Val, both of whom were associated with the repressive policies of St. Pius X. A Roman "joke" (that is, a witticism with a point) said that Merry del Val, son of the Spanish ambassador to London, could never be beatified, for then there would be no one to blame for Pius X's mistakes.

Now patriarch of Venice, La Fontaine had been prefect of the Consistorial Congregation and therefore Grand Inquisitor supreme under Pius X. Among his victims or near-misses was the young Angelo Roncalli, the future Pope John XXIII. Merry del Val, educated in England during his father's term as ambassador, had been St. Pius's secretary of state at the age of thirty-five. To call them conservatives would be an understatement. But the reason they were excommunicated was that they tried to make a deal with Achille Ratti, who, after a hesitant start, soon became the favorite. He could have their votes, they intimated, provided he did not have Pietro Gasparri as secretary of state.

Gasparri, principal author of the Code of Canon Law, which improbably appeared in 1917, had been Benedict XV's secretary of state. Continuity suggested he would be an obvious choice for the succession. But the supporters of Pius X, still miffed by the "mistake" of 1914, were resolved to block Gasparri. In this conclave, much of the hard work took place during the *Novemdiales,* or nine days of mourning that precede the locking up in the Apostolic Palace. Secrecy at this point is not always watertight.

Even though the Austro-Hungarian Empire had ceased

to exist, fragmented into a multiplicity of small states, Austria still aspired to play a role in the conclave. Vienna, by now a very large head on a very small body, shrewdly appointed the Baron Ludwig von Pastor as its ambassador. Since Leopold von Ranke in the nineteenth century, nobody knew more about the papacy than von Pastor. His *History of the Popes* remains indispensable. There was still, he held, a role for Austria in a conclave. It was the last time anyone could cherish this illusion.

On January 27, 1922, von Pastor met Cardinal Piffl off the train from Vienna. The German-speaking cardinals met for a noncommittal *tour d'horizon*. Piffl's diary records the result of their eve-of-conclave discussions: "Five qualities seem to be required of the new pope: (1) A deep religious life. (2) a diplomat. (3) a learned man. (4) a man well versed in politics. (5) a correct attitude toward the Italian government."[7] That seemed to mean someone who was prepared to work for reconciliation with Italy and so to solve the "Roman Question"—that is, what to do about the lost Papal States.

As often happens, it was easier to sketch out a job description for the papacy than to find a candidate to realize it. The Dutch Cardinal William Van Rossum, longtime resident in Rome, prefect of the Congregation Propaganda Fide (that is, missions; now the Congregation for the Evangelization of Peoples), otherwise known as the "red pope," was the main *grande elettore*.

In his view the time had come for a non-Italian pope. He was thinking not of himself, but of Merry del Val. Though somewhat premature, the idea was not totally absurd. Its weakness was that, after a lifetime in Rome, non-Italian cardinals lost their national identity and became "more Italian than the Italians." This was certainly true of Merry del Val, who appeared as little more than a clone of Pius X, who had promoted him from nothing. Once again the two American cardinals, William H. O'Connell of Boston and Dennis Dougherty, archbishop of Philadelphia, were mortified to arrive at Rome's Termini station half an hour after the pope had been elected.[8]

MORAL: Do not see cardinals as idealistic dreamers, ignorant of the mechanisms of power.

Ratti took the name of Pius XI and personified the Church of his period: tough-minded, unyielding, and vigorous in the defense of the institutional rights of the Church in the age of dictators.

The conclave of March 1939 was the briefest and most predictable of the century so far. After the Munich crisis of the previous autumn, war was inevitable. The usual debate about a "spiritual" or a "diplomatic" pope was settled in favor of the most experienced and brilliant diplomat available, Roman-born Eugenio Pacelli, his predecessor's secretary of state since 1929. He had been nuncio in Bavaria and Berlin, where he learned German and read Goethe to perfect his style. He traveled widely—and by airplane—and lunched with President Franklin D. Roosevelt. On this slender basis he was widely considered a "modern" man.

However, Pacelli's election was not a foregone conclusion. The Italian cardinals thought his temperament suspect—a bag of nervous hesitations. His colleague in the Secretariat of State Domenico Tardini put this nicely: "He was by temperament gentle and rather shy. He wasn't a fighter. . . . His great goodness led him to wish to please everyone, and to prefer the path of gentleness to that of severity, to persuade rather than to impose. That explains, if anything does, his silences."[9] It also explains why fourteen cardinals of the Roman Curia obstinately refused to vote for him, even though he had it in the bag. They knew him better than foreigners did who were dazzled at that time by his diplomatic brilliance, before later doubts crept in about his failure to take a stand against Nazism.

Pius XII was, in short, not a pope for wartime, when, as the British minister said, one needed not a *Pastor Angelicus* ("angelic pastor")—the Malachy-prompted name—but a *Leo Furibundus* ("a raging lion"). The see of New York was vacant. One of the first and most fateful acts of Pius XII was to appoint Francis J. Spellman archbishop of New York.[10]

MORAL: Be careful about popes who say "I don't want collaborators, but executants."

As Pius XII, Pacelli had a long and increasingly authoritarian reign. Despite popular legend, he was not theologically well educated. If anything, he was a canon lawyer. He tried to remedy his deficiencies by staying up late at night studying, say, the gas industry from encyclopedias, in preparation for his next morning's address.

In theology he was a *terrible simplificateur*. Whatever appeared to depart from "the deposit of faith" was anathema. He beatified and canonized Pius X. It was enough for the French Dominican Réginald Garrigou-Lagrange to tell him that the deposit of faith was being gnawed away by French Jesuits and Dominicans for him to act. *Humani Generis* condemned them in 1950. It was the last theological witch-hunt of the century—so far. Garrigou-Lagrange, meanwhile, was supervising the thesis on "Faith in St. John of the Cross" written by the brilliant twenty-seven-year-old Polish priest Karol Wojtyla.

Pius XII nearly died in 1954. Cardinals packed their bags, diplomats prepared their memos, journalists speculated. The Italian ambassador to the Holy See, Dr. Mameli, wrote a revealing report admirably summing up what "informed sources" were saying at the time.

Mameli said that to penetrate the thickets of the next conclave, three questions had to be faced:

Papa italiano o Papa straniero? An Italian or a foreigner?
Papa politico o Papa religioso? A political or a religious pope?
Starà nella media dell'età o no? A middle-aged pope or not?[11]

Mameli did not expect the election of a "young pope." The composition of the college of cardinals suggested that they would not buy any such idea. "An older pope would be more acceptable to them, especially if the idea of a *transitional pontificate* came to be accepted."

The Italian ambassador, having unknowingly provided the principle that would govern the conclave that actually did take place in 1958, then mooted names. He left aside Giuseppe Siri (why? too young? too close to Pius XII?) and offered a classic list of three "safe" men (Alfredo Ottaviani, Giacomo Lercaro, Ernesto Ruffini). But he added that "outsiders" (in English) like Mimmi could come through. His most "prophetic" remark came in an aside: "If the idea of a 'diplomatic' Pope prevails, then there are various nuncios created in the last consistory [of 1953] who are between seventy and seventy-three. In some circles the name of Roncalli, Patriarch of Venice, is mentioned, as bringing together the two qualities of 'diplomat' and 'religious.'" Add his "transitional" quality—the fact that he would not be around for very long—and his election seems almost inevitable.

Mameli hit another nail on the head when he suggested that Roncalli's rival could well be Gregory Peter Agagianian, the Armenian prefect of Propaganda Fide. But he was only a "token" foreigner, having been thoroughly romanized. "We two went up and down like two chickpeas in a pot,"[12] said Pope John afterward.

Angelo Roncalli, who would emerge from the 1958 conclave as pope, was concerned about Pius XII's illness in 1954, but even more worried by Gaston Bardet, a French would-be prophet who had sent him a proof copy of his latest book. Roncalli, now patriarch of Venice, replied that this "mish-mash of predictions bears all the marks of the 'spirit of confusion'"—in other words it came from the devil. In January 1955, Roncalli wrote to his sister, Maria: "Some mad Frenchman, who has revelations and second sight, has even given the name I will take when they make me pope. Mad, mad the whole lot of them. I'm thinking rather of death. I have a full program of work for this year and also for next year."[13] All well and good: but *what name* did the Frenchman say he would take? We can lay a bet on it being John. *Vocabor Johannes* ("I will be called John") was a surprise, because John was a name associated with "bad" popes and not used since the fourteenth century.

The conclave in 1958, however, was the first at which an American cardinal was considered seriously *papabile*. Francis J. Spellman thought he still had a chance. This was an illusion, as his biographer, John Cooney, explains: "Another strike against Spellman was his nationality. An American pope would give credence to Communist claims that the Vatican was the tool of the United States."[14] He was also regarded as too "political" and "unspiritual." In the end, the "American era" resulted in the building of the North American College and the Villa Stritch as the residence for Americans working in the Curia.

MORAL: The bookies get it wrong, and the Holy Spirit has its little jokes—the transitional pope became the pope of the Church's transition.

Having a devoted a whole chapter to the 1963 conclave in *Paul VI: The First Modern Pope,* I can be brief on it here. Giovanni Battista Montini, archbishop of Milan, was expected to win, and did. The contest was fierce. His principal rival was Cardinal Giacomo Lercaro, archbishop of Bologna, who had undergone a startling conversion in the pontificate of

Pope John. The bookmakers' odds fluctuated wildly. Bernard Pawley, the first permanent Anglican representative in Rome, reported in an unpublished paper to the archbishops of Canterbury and York:

> *Montini is played down while Lercaro is played up in his place. In public opinion Confalonieri the favorite. Urbani of Venice and Costaldo of Naples increasingly canvassed. So put them on a "long list.". . . In the present state of tension, nobody will get the candidate they really want, and they will have to agree on a "third man."*[15]

He was learning the lingo, if not the ropes, fast. Every speculator needs a "long list" and a "short list," and a "third man" as a "compromise candidate" to break the deadlock. But these considerations apart, Pawley's presence and remarks show how important papal conclaves have become for all Christians.

The fact that a "third man" was not needed in 1963 does not mean that it was not a close run. At one point Cardinal Gustavo Testa, a fat friend of Pope John from Bergamo, lost his temper and told his neighbor, in a stage whisper loud enough to be heard all round the Sistine Chapel, that "they should stop their squalid maneuverings and consider the good of the Church." This broke the rules. Voting should be done in silence. But Testa was right. When it was all over, he said: "Hair-raising things happened in this conclave—I will have to ask the pope's permission to speak abut them." He never did.

Anyway, Montini scraped home on the sixth ballot, gaining only two more votes than the required fifty-seven. As Cardinal Lercaro knelt before him, Paul VI said to him: "So that is the way life goes, Your Eminence. You should really be sitting here now."

MORAL: In this case it was drawn by the new pope himself: after the "hair-raising things"—attempts to strike deals and determine the future course of the Second Vatican Council—Paul VI determined to reform the rules of the conclave. How he did that, and what its effects were, will be the subject of the next chapter.

THREE

How the Conclave Reforms Work

Paul VI would have been a reforming pope even if Vatican II had never happened. What he chiefly wanted to reform was the Roman Curia, the bureaucracy by which the pope administers the Church. In 1942, in the darkest days of the war, he told Galeazzo Ciano, Mussolini's son-in-law and foreign minister, that the Roman Curia would have to lose its "Italian" character and be properly internationalized.

One way to do this would have been to have had more Americans in high curial places. After the death of Cardinal Luigi Maglione in August 1944, Pius XII desperately wanted Cardinal Francis J. Spellman, archbishop of New York, to succeed him as secretary of state. Spellman's diary recalls how, with tears in his eyes, Pius XII confided this intention to him in September 1944. But it would have to wait, for, with the war not yet over, it would never do for a cardinal from one of the belligerents to become secretary of state.

In the meantime, "Vessels," the espionage service that was the ancestor of the CIA, discovered this scheme and put it about, thus ruining it. Heartbroken at the failure of his plan, which would in his mind have signaled a new "American era" in the Church, Pius XII determined not to appoint a secretary of state at all.

The man left in charge was Montini. He knew that to reform the Curia was to reform the papacy. In 1950 he mused aloud with Riccardo Lombardi, S.J., on the need for a much simplified and more evangelical papacy. He outlined his vision of a pope based at the cathedral church of the bishop of Rome, St. John Lateran:

> *Let the Pope leave the Vatican with all those in it, let him leave them with their stipends and go off, at least for certain periods, to St. John Lateran; there he would live with his seminarians, with his people, with a new ritual. . . . He could return to the Vatican from time to time. And in St. John Lateran he would begin a new way of governing the Church, like Peter who was a poor man.[1]*

It is facile to point out that, as pope, Montini did not follow his own advice. Any pope works within certain constraints.

Yet he did his best to reform the Curia inherited from Pius XII and largely left intact by John XXIII. The crucial point was to impose a retirement age on cardinals. Without it, cardinals behaved like medieval barons, able to go on empire building until they died. Paul VI changed all that with *Regimini Ecclesiae* of 1967. Moreover, he struck another blow against gerontocracy by insisting that all offices should last for not more than five years, be renewable only once, and be relinquished on the accession of a new pope.

Paul's reforming streak was enormously strengthened by Vatican II. Every role and task in the Church was held up for inspection and marked for renewal: priest, layperson, religious, bishop, missionary. But there were two exceptions: neither the papal office itself nor the college of cardinals came under scrutiny. The best, and probably the only, way in which he could reform the papacy was by the manner in which he exercised it. Pope John modified the practice of the papacy whatever the theory, refusing, for example, the notion of producing "infallible" statements. Paul did the same, though in more unobtrusive ways, making himself a leader in ecumenical affairs and his office a possible rallying point for the unity of all Christians.

The college of cardinals was a fit subject for reform. Medieval creations with no scriptural foundation, cardinals stuck out like sore thumbs in the era of collegiality. Where was the Church? Vatican II taught that the Church existed in and through local congregations, the church in Harlem or the church in Westminster. This was a return to New Testament usage, where *church* was as often plural as singular: the churches of Ephesus and Corinth, and the seven churches of Asia mentioned in the Apocalypse, made up the one Church that was the Body of Christ. That was an important Vatican II rediscovery.

It implied that the bishops, as heads of the local churches, were inserted into the universal Church through their communion with the Bishop of Rome, who inherited from Peter the primacy. So the pope (not a theological title) presides over the whole assembly of charity. It is not just a matter of adding up the local churches. All the bishops of the world form a college, or team, with their president. This the council called "collegiality."

In this scheme the key, indeed, essential, players were bishops and archbishops; but cardinals did not fit in. A common theological opinion summed up by René Laurentin held that "it was an anomaly, if not a scandal, that the episcopal college existing by divine right has so very little part in the government of the Church, while the college of cardinals enjoys all the power, privileges, precedence and tenure."[2]

Bishop Christopher Butler, former abbot of Downside, went further still. The logic of Vatican II suggested that, on the death of a pope, authority in the Church devolved upon the college of bishops. So if the college of cardinals enjoyed the privilege of being the sole electors of the pope, they did so only by virtue of some kind of delegation from the world's bishops.[3] Cardinal Léon-Joseph Suenens drew the conclusion that it would be more appropriate for the conclave to be made up of presidents of episcopal conferences, since they formed the truly collegial group representing the whole Church.

Paul VI was sensitive to these arguments, though awed and perhaps alarmed at the prospect of departing from a precedent nearly a thousand years old. Rather than respond directly, he took a preliminary step. On November 21, 1970, he launched his first missile at the college of cardinals. It took the form of the decree *Ingravescentem Aetatem*. It declared that cardinals over eighty could not take part in a conclave. This effectively pensioned them off.

As Paul VI, now aged seventy-three, set off for his last papal journey to the Philippines and Australia, ousted cardinals like Alfredo Ottaviani, eighty, and Eugène Tisserant, eighty-six, went on Italian television and waxed formidably indignant. Ottaviani, the baker's son from Trastevere, by now almost totally blind, for so many years the chief watchdog of orthodoxy at the Holy Office, quivered his mighty jowls at the indignity of it all. The papal decision, he spluttered, was "absolutely unheard of, arbitrary, revolutionary, in contempt of a centuries-old tradition." Tisserant, a French cavalry officer in the World War I, conducted his last campaign with panache. He complained that the pope was practicing "moral euthanasia." Both Tisserant and Ottaviani asked what would happen when the Holy Father himself reached eighty. If the over-eighties were deemed incapable of electing a pope, someone over eighty could surely not be considered capable of exercising the office itself.

They had a point. An eighty-year-old pope would have to resign. At this date, it may be surmised, Paul VI did not expect to live to eighty. Tisserant, solid as a rock, said he would outlive Paul VI and looked forward to reaching one hundred in 1985. (In fact, he died some fifteen months later, on February 21, 1972.)

Excluding the over-eighties was an important precedent. It meant that the composition of the conclave was not immutable: it was not set in stone. In such matters small changes can be as significant as big ones. Ottaviani was right to say that this was a revolutionary decision.

But could Paul VI go further and embrace the Suenens proposal of making the Extraordinary Synod the electoral body? Such an assembly was held in 1969 to deal with the problems that arose after Paul VI rejected artificial birth control in *Humanae Vitae*. It was made up of presidents of episcopal conferences. Some of them happened to be cardinals, but not all were. Could this—should this—be the body to make up the conclave? Some such project was certainly "being studied."

However, on March 5, 1973, addressing the latest batch of cardinals, Paul produced a watered-down version of this plan. The college of cardinals would remain the electoral body. But there would be added to it the fifteen members of the Synod Council (a body set up by the 1971 synod), twelve of whom were elected by their peers (three per continent). A few noncardinals would thus be involved. It would also be good to include Oriental patriarchs.[4]

This proposal created an even greater furor among the Italian cardinals than the exclusion of the over-eighties.

Cardinal Giuseppe Siri, of Genoa, a possible pope in all the conclaves of the second half of the century, argued against it in an audience with Paul VI lasting an hour and a half:

> *It was like a game of ping-pong; he listened to my arguments and countered with his own dialectic. I held back till the end one last objection: it was a mistake to put on the same level cardinals who are named by the pope and bishops who are appointed in a different way.*
>
> *Cardinals are answerable to no one, while bishops have to account for their decisions. So they can be easily "conditioned." This term alarmed Paul VI. "Very well," he said, "it will be the sacred college and it alone that will elect the pope." Then I took his hand, kissed his ring, and fled. If I had gone on any more, he would have flung an ash-tray at my head.[5]*

Was Siri the smoker? A large pinch of salt should be taken with this story. Siri typically overestimated his own influence. The idea that cardinals are more genuinely independent than bishops is true only if the bishops desperately want to become cardinals and are thus paralyzed by caution.

Yet after wavering on this question, Paul VI's new legislation, contained in the apostolic constitution *Romano Pontifici Eligendo*, officially dated October 1, 1975, confined the election to cardinals under eighty. It innovated only in its rigor about secrecy, its mania for security inspections, and the terrifying oaths it imposed. Above all, it insisted that cardinals should normally go into the conclave alone, unless they needed serious medical assistance, in which case they had to prove it. In the previous more relaxed tradition, approved by Pope John, cardinals were allowed to take in a couple of friends as *conclavistas* and a third if they were ill.

In 1958 Cardinal Francis J. Spellman took in two junior

aides. One of them, George A. Schlichte, has left an account of what happened:

> *Spellman sat on the housing committee. We occupied half of a completely furnished apartment with two baths. The ecclesiastical occupant had gotten bumped because he happened to reside within the conclave area. Cardinal Pizzardo and his one lay assistant occupied one room each, as did Spellman and his secretary. I slept in a cot in the dining room and stocked up the refrigerator with extras on the morning of the lock-up. I saw cardinals with quarters made by curtains at the ends of corridors and under stairways. All the cardinals ate meals at one oval table. The rest of us ate at long tables in a nearby room. After the second morning Spellman announced that he could take these cardinals at lunch and supper but not for breakfast. I then boiled the eggs.[6]*

Paul put a stop to this cheerful informality. The cardinals would be on their own before God. While in conclave they were on retreat.

Only the minimum number of necessary officials were allowed in to arrange for liturgies and confessions, medical attention and material needs, to be chosen by the majority of the cardinals on the proposal of the *camerlengo* and his three cardinal assistants. With hangers-on eliminated, those allowed in have to take an oath of secrecy. Clearly, the idea was to make the next conclave as watertight as possible.

But this intention was frustrated by another important clause. The over-eighties were excluded from the conclave: there was no going back on that. But they were not excluded, indeed they were invited, to the discussions preceding the entry into the conclave known as "General Congregations." Paul VI prescribed that at least fifteen and not more than twenty days should elapse between the death of a pope and the entry into the conclave. Cardinals would join in the General Congregations just as soon as they arrived at Rome's Leonardo da Vinci airport. Many of them, preoccupied with their pastoral work, would not feel a great sense of urgency. They would not make haste.

Those cardinals already in place in Rome would have an advantage in these early stages. Even if they did not have undue influence—which cannot be excluded—they would watch with great keenness an event from which they felt most unjustly excluded. Cardinal Carlo Confalonieri, a *conclavista* in 1922 when Pius XI was elected, observed the "smokes" of 1978 from his rooftop garden. Not to tell him, in the strictest confidence of course, how the voting went would be cruel indeed. But since he was not in the conclave, he was not under oath.

But *Romano Pontifici Eligendo* was not the last word on the operation of the conclave. John Paul II updated the rules in his apostolic constitution *Universi Dominici Gregis*, dated February 22, 1996. He abolished any provision for election by acclamation or by any means other than secret ballot. The procedure is now as follows.

A votive Mass *Pro Eligendo Papa* will be held not less than fifteen and not more than twenty days after the death. That same afternoon the cardinals will meet in the Pauline Chapel, inside the Apostolic Palace, and, chanting the *Veni Creator* ("Come Holy Spirit"), they will process to the Sistine Chapel. They will take an oath of secrecy, and, at the cry *Extra omnes* ("Everybody out"), all those not taking part in the conclave will leave. On that first afternoon, the first ballot may be held, though this is not compulsory. After that, there will normally be two ballots each morning and two each afternoon.

The system of voting, already described in the Prelude, seems to have been devised with the aim of making the procedure take as long as possible. More time for thought. Each cardinal comes up to the altar, declares before God the integrity of his voting intention, places the folded ballot on the paten, tips it into the chalice, bows, and returns. Watching that 120 times over must get rather boring, even on the first ballot.

After that the counting is just as cumbersome. First the total number of votes cast must be counted. If the total is not the same as the number of cardinals present, all the ballots must be burned and the procedure begun all over again. If the number is right, the ballots may be opened. The first scrutineer unfolds a paper, notes down the name, and passes it on to the second scrutineer, who notes down the name and passes it to the third scrutineer, who reads it aloud in a clear voice. All the cardinals present can then note it down on their own sheets specially provided for the purpose. The third scrutineer himself writes down the name, and then pierces the ballot paper with a needle through the first printed word, *Eligo*, until all the ballots are threaded together and can be tied up with a knot.

The votes of any cardinals too ill to come to the Sistine Chapel are collected from their bedsides in the Santa Marta, in boxes with a slit in the top. As if three scrutineers were not enough, there are also three "revisers," who have to check the work of the scrutineers on every ballot. If no one is elected by the necessary two-thirds majority, the whole procedure is repeated for a second vote, which takes place at once. Then all the ballots, together with all the note sheets of the individual cardinals, are burned.

Meanwhile the Roman crowds have gathered in the Piazza San Pietro, full of excited anticipation as they strain their eyes at the distant chimney to see which color smoke comes out. Additives to the fire are supposed to ensure that the smoke comes out black when there is no pope and white when there has been a successful election, but experience has shown it is not always easy to tell the difference. The emeritus archbishop of Durban, South Africa, Denis E. Hurley, wrote in a letter that on the election of Pius XII he was watching the thin trail of smoke creeping from the Sistine Chapel chimney and "found it difficult to make out whether the smoke was white or not" because it was "already dusk at 5:45 P.M. on the second day of March. I remember commenting that people thousands of miles away from St. Peter's knew of the successful election before those of us standing puzzled in the Piazza."[7]

The crowd disperses rapidly once it is satisfied that the smoke is black, but if it is white, the numbers swell rapidly as the word gets around the city. The huge square will be teeming, and the crowds will spill well down the Via della Conciliazione. Their enthusiasm will know no bounds as they wait for the new pope to be introduced to them over powerful loudspeakers from the balcony above the entrance to St. Peter's.

But before that point is reached, there may be several days of black smoke. Indeed, Pope John Paul II's major innovation in *Universi Dominici Gregis* could tempt some determined cardinals to stick out long enough to be able to force a change in the rules, so they can get through a candidate who obtains more than half but less than two-thirds of the votes. The new rule is complicated, but goes like this. "After balloting has been carried out for three days" in the form described, "voting is to be suspended for a maximum of one day" to allow a pause for prayer, discussion, and a spiritual exhortation. "Voting is then resumed in the usual manner, and after seven ballots, if the election has not taken place, there is another pause." There is "another series of seven ballots," followed by "a further pause for prayer, discussion, and an exhortation." And then voting continues for another seven ballots.

If we leave aside the optional vote on the first afternoon, the cardinals will now appear to have been thirteen days inside the conclave and to have held thirty ballots. At this point,

> the cardinal electors shall be invited by the camerlengo to express an opinion about the manner of proceeding. The election will then proceed in accordance with what the absolute majority of the electors decides. Nevertheless, there can be no waiving of the requirement that a valid election takes place only by an absolute majority of the votes or else by voting only on the two names which in the ballot immediately preceding have received the greatest number of votes; also in this second case only an absolute majority is required. (p. 75)

Although this nontraditional procedure is clearly intended to come into effect only in extreme circumstances to break a deadlock, the very fact that such provision is made means that a determined majority short of the two-thirds could force through their man simply by holding out long enough.

The remaining articles of *Universi Dominici Gregis* inflict excommunication on those who try to buy votes or to convey into the conclave a veto or any other kind of influence from any secular authority. Pacts, promises, or agreements conditional on election are "null and void," though the intention is not to forbid "the exchange of views concerning the election." Cardinal electors are not to be guided "by friendship or aversion" or "by the suggestions of the mass media," but should have

> before their eyes solely the glory of God and the good of the Church, and, having prayed for divine assistance, they shall give their vote to the person, even outside the College of Cardinals, who in their judgment is most suited to govern the universal Church in a fruitful and beneficial way. (p. 83)

Meanwhile the election of a pope is "in a certain sense an act of the whole Church" in that everyone "should persevere with one heart in prayer" following the example of the first Christian community before Pentecost. The cardinals who are excluded by being over eighty are invited to "lead the prayer of the People of God, whether gathered in the patriarchal basilicas of the city of Rome or in places of worship in other particular churches," and so can "participate in an effective and real way" in the process.

Finally, the one elected is to be asked by the dean of the college, at present Cardinal Bernardin Gantin, if he accepts his election. He is urged to say yes, and at that point he is immediately the Bishop of Rome. Then he is asked, "By what name do you wish to be called?" The cardinal electors approach to pay their homage, and then the new pope is presented to the people from the balcony, by Gantin, and he gives them his first *Urbi et Orbi* blessing.

Although the most substantial change from previous regulations is in the softening of the two-thirds rule, the most evident alteration in the experience of the cardinals will be their new accommodations in the Santa Marta. Back in 1978, it was a very different affair. The oldest and most fragile cardinals were lodged next to the Sistine Chapel and the Sala Borgia, where meals were taken; the others were assigned rooms by lot the previous day. There were great differences between the "cells." Not much had changed since 1958. Some were poky little offices, tucked away in odd corners, with discolored patches on the walls where charts or pictures had been removed. Others were lodged in vast Renaissance reception rooms, where the ceilings were forty feet high and the cardinal, after putting out his chandelier for the night, would have to pick his way nimbly around vast tables and capacious sofas.

But whether in a dingy office or a marble hall, the equipment was modest and standardized: a bed borrowed from the infirmary of Propaganda Fide (the missionary college); a red-shaded lamp too faint to read a breviary by; a wash-basin, soap (Donge of Paris), a bucket for slops, and a packet of tissues; a writing table with notepaper and an ash-tray; a prie-dieu. All that spartan simplicity was designed to prevent a long conclave, especially in the summer. The impression of living in an "airless tomb," as Cardinal Siri called it in 1978, will change utterly at the next election, now that the Santa Marta has been built. And that will make it much more possible for the cardinals to stick out a long conclave, perhaps one long enough to allow them to get to the end of the second week, when the two-thirds rule can be dropped and a pope can be elected with no more than an absolute majority.

However, in August 1978 the austere monastic seclusion lasted only a day. The cardinals went in on the afternoon of August 25, and the conclave was all over by the evening of August 26. Albino Luciani, patriarch of Venice, emerged as pope and invented the double-barreled name John Paul name to honor both his predecessors. The swiftness of the election—there is a scholarly dispute about whether there were three or four ballots—brought out the importance of the preconclave discussions in preparing for the conclave.

After the election, the eighty-five-year-old Cardinal Carlo Confalonieri was asked on Italian television whether he was surprised:

> *It was certainly not a surprise for me or the other cardinals. The name of Cardinal Luciani was one that had attracted the attention of the cardinal electors in the last days of the precon-clave period. . . . I have to admit that, at the start, a number of cardinals did not know him well, but this was no longer so after the various daily meetings held under my presidency.*

Quite clearly, he had worked for "his" candidate. So the sixteen over-eighties, mostly Romans like Confalonieri, were without a vote, but not without influence. The preconclave meetings had a determining role in fixing what the cardinals were looking for and in their getting to know each other.

The time was spent listening to official reports from the Secretariat of State about the situation of the Church. There was a brief furor at the vagueness of the financial report presented by Cardinal Egidio Vagnozzi, formerly apostolic delegate in Washington. Cardinal Jean Villot, secretary of state and *camerlengo*, ordered him to omit detailed references to shares and property on the grounds that "the African cardinals would not understand these matters and would draw God knows what conclusions."[8] This was politically incorrect. Cardinal Pietro Palazzini demanded to know why the Institute of Religious Works (IOR), commonly known as the Vatican Bank and headed by Archbishop Paul C. Marcinkus, native of Cicero, Illinois, had not been mentioned. Vagnozzi batted that back. It was treacherous terrain.

There were 111 cardinals—more than ever before. "How many fresh faces there are," remarked Cardinal Stefan Wyszynski, primate of Poland, to the cardinal archbishop of Kraków, Karol Wojtyla. Wyszynski, at seventy-eight too old to be a candidate, presented a report in which he contrasted the situation in Poland, where the Church had gained more concessions from the Communists than anywhere else, with the pitiable state of churches where bishops had been imposed by the regime. This brought a brisk riposte from the Hungarian Cardinal László Lékai (the man who had replaced Cardinal Jozsef Mindszenty), who saw some merit in Marxism.

Wyszynski's report was critical of Paul VI's *Ostpolitik*, which the Polish bishops had never liked. They found it too feeble and compromising, easy prey for ruthless Communists. They wanted a tougher, more resolute approach. It was easy to pass from being critical of Paul's *Ostpolitik* to being critical of him generally. On the right, he was regarded as hesitant and vacillating, making his mind up too late or not at all on contraception, clerical celibacy, religious life, and the other postconciliar problems. The critics of Paul VI were dubbed the "Roman party."

Their candidate was Cardinal Giuseppe Siri, archbishop of Genoa since 1946. Once described as "the archconservatives' archconservative," he thought the pontificate of Pope John XXIII a disaster for the Church (though he later relented before the beatification investigation) and resisted Vatican II changes. Curial cardinals knew that they were out of the reckoning, because after Vatican II the emphasis was on pastoral rather than bureaucratic experience. Siri could claim abundant pastoral experience in Genoa. He would be just the man to take a firm grip on the rudder of Peter's barque.

Indeed, he volunteered for the job. In the second of the mourning sermons, Siri reminded the cardinals that the "Holy Spirit" had not abolished their responsibility: "I think I have a duty to warn my fellow cardinals of the task that is before them and which they cannot elude by saying, 'This is what the Holy Spirit thinks.' Nor should they abandon themselves, without toil and suffering, to their first impulse or to unreasonable suggestions." What on earth did he mean? No doubt he had in mind the "pressures" being put on the conclave by theologians and journalists who wanted a pastoral pope, committed to Vatican II, who could also smile. The cardinals should disdain such emotional claptrap and vote for the man of experience, himself.

This suggestion alarmed the majority of the cardinals. They might be critical of some of Paul VI's hesitations, but that did not mean regarding Vatican II as misguided. But who could carry this standard? Cardinal Sergio Pignedoli, a man of great charm and international friendships, seemed a likely runner. But he was a curialist, he was "too close" to Paul VI (he had been his auxiliary in Milan), and he allegedly had made a famous gaffe in Libya.

The name of Albino Luciani, patriarch of Venice, began to be heard. He would be the candidate of continuity with Paul VI, but "continuity with a smile." While the press pool was visiting the conclave area on the eve of the conclave, an old friend who shall be called Monsignor Ossobuco passed by. "I cannot tell you who will be pope," he said. "No one can; but ask yourself, Who is Cardinal Benelli's candidate?" Giovanni Benelli had been Paul VI's right-hand man and closest colleague. Though it broke his heart, Paul sent Benelli to Florence in June 1977 as archbishop and made him a cardinal so that he could avoid Paul's own fate in 1954: he had been sent to Milan as archbishop, but without a cardinal's hat, so he missed the conclave of 1958.

Now Benelli would be the kingmaker rather than the king, the *grande elettore*. From his vantage point as *sostituto* ("substitute") to Paul VI, Benelli knew the college of cardinals better than anyone. He was an implacable opponent of Siri. He had seen Luciani at work among the northern Italian bishops and saw he was friendly and able, with great skills in communication. If an Italian pastoral bishop was wanted, he was the logical candidate.

Chance friendships also helped Luciani. Cardinal Paulo Evaristo Arns, archbishop of São Paulo, Brazil, was made a cardinal in 1973 at the same time. Arns says they talked about the Church of the poor and the Third World. Another Brazilian Franciscan, Cardinal Aloísio Lorscheider, archbishop of Fortaleza, invited Luciani to Brazil in 1976 to deal with the pastoral problems of Italian workers. Luciani was better known in Latin America, where his words were reported in the press, than even in Italy. On his return from Brazil in 1976 Luciani told a Venetian priest that he would be happy to see Lorscheider as pope. "He is a man of faith and culture," he said, "and he has a good knowledge of Italy and of Italian." He then added: "The time has come to chose a pope from the Third World."

In that he proved mistaken. But by the time of the conclave, Lorscheider's view was that if it was somewhat premature to expect a pope from the Third World, then someone who "loved the Third World" was the next best thing. None of this guaranteed his election, and one cannot speak of collusion in advance.

The proof is that the first ballot on the morning of August 26 revealed a vast scatter of names. The leaders were these:

25 Siri, Giuseppe
23 Luciani, Albino
18 Pignedoli, Sergio
 9 Baggio, Sebastiano
 8 König, Franz

The Sistine Chapel chimney emitted black or at least grayish smoke. The second ballot followed immediately. Siri lost only one vote, Pignedoli only three, but nearly all the votes for individual candidates drifted to Luciani, who gained thirty. The leaders in the second ballot were:

53 Luciani, Albino
24 Siri, Giuseppe
15 Pignedoli, Sergio
 4 Wojtyla, Karol

With hindsight, the appearance of Wojtyla is significant. If the top "non-Italian," König, dropped out, then someone was trying to say that the next "non-Italian" in the line was the cardinal archbishop of Kraków.

But there was no time to think of that. As they came out of the Sistine Chapel, the Hungarian Lékai remarked to Luciani: "Your votes are increasing." To which the patriarch of Venice, perhaps thinking of the heat in the Apostolic Palace, replied: "It's just a summer shower." It was time for lunch, and time to consult.

The next ballot was not till 4:30 in the afternoon. There was a meeting in the cell (as the rooms were quaintly called) of Cardinal Vincente Enrique y Tarancón, archbishop of Madrid. Present were all the European "progressives"— Suenens, Alfrink of Utrecht, König, but they were joined by others, like the Oxford-educated Pakistani Joseph Cordeiro, for instance. "We talked together," said Enrique y Tarancón, "because we weren't quite sure where we were going." But in fact they were now in the clear.

Sources argue about whether there were two more ballots or only one. *Civiltà Cattolica* prudently remarked that "Pope John Paul was elected, it *seems,* on the third ballot." Why that cautious "it seems" from this usually so assured review? The best hypothesis is that Luciani, though he had more than the seventy-five votes needed on the third ballot, was hesitant to accept. The following story confirms that. As Siri went with Villot and Felici to put to him the formal question, "Do you accept?" Baggio tugged at his sleeve. "Advise him to take the name Eugene," said Baggio, "because the last Venetian Pope was Eugene IV." "This is not the right moment to be talking about names," Siri replied, "when we don't even know he will accept."

Suppose that Luciani, knowing perfectly well that the rebel conservative Archbishop Marcel Lefebvre had declared in advance he would reject any candidate emerging from a conclave from which the over-eighties were absent, then

called for a "confirming" vote to put to rest any such juridical doubts. That would explain the confusion about whether
he was elected on the third or the fourth ballot. It would
also explain why the final ballot was "almost by acclamation"
(as Vatican Radio remarked). Cardinal Joseph Höffner of
Cologne said: "There was no need to count the names,
because the only name read out by the scrutineers was that
of Luciani." Höffner also disclosed that the pope's first
words, on taking his seat before the altar, were: "God will for-
give you for what you have done to me." They needed forgiveness, for they had, all unwittingly, put him at great risk of
his life. But this knowledge came only with hindsight: his
anxious temperament and ignorance of the Roman Curia—
he spent much time flicking through the pages of the
Annuario Pontificio discovering who was who—offset the
charm of his smile. But, most of all, no attention had been
paid to his state of health. It was enough that at sixty-five he
was in the right age bracket and seemed good for another
ten years.

This was gravely mistaken. John Paul I lasted just thirty-
three days (August 26 to September 28). But there is no
need to resort to conspiracy theories or murder plots. John
Cornwell's verdict in *A Thief in the Night* is surely right: "John
Paul almost certainly died of a pulmonary embolus due to a
condition of abnormal coagularity of the blood. He required
rest and monitored medication. If these had been prescribed
he would almost certainly have survived. The warnings of a
mortal illness were clear for all to see; the signs were
ignored."[9]

Villot, still secretary of state and once again *camerlengo*,
devoted some time in the General Congregations to the circumstances of Pope John Paul's death. He admitted that the
Vatican press office, in saying that John Paul I was discovered by Father John Magee and that he had been reading

The Imitation of Christ, had given misleading information. But the idea, proposed by Cardinal Confalonieri, that they should produce a collegial statement on the death of John Paul I was rejected: such matters escaped their competence.[10] They could not, in any case, "create facts."

The mood in the October 1978 conclave was very different from that in August. There was an atmosphere of crisis in the air. *L'Osservatore Romano*, the Vatican daily, hinted at the possibility of a third world war. Rockets were raining down on the Christians of Lebanon. The Red Brigades were again a factor to be reckoned with in Italy. This approach—called by Italians the "strategy of tension"—suggested that a strong pope of great doctrinal firmness was called for.

The *Novemdiales* sermons all pointed in the same direction. They produced an edited version in which John Paul I's liberal impulses were screened out and he was presented as a "pope of restoration." According to Confalonieri, he was a "meteor which unexpectedly lights up the heavens, and then disappears." He had stressed "the integrity of doctrine, the perfection of Christian life, and the great discipline of the Church." This, he intimated, was what drew the vast crowds to the Wednesday audiences, and not the superficial freshness of his style and his famous smile. According to Cardinal Siri, "John Paul I spoke with great simplicity on the firmness of Catholic doctrine, on ecclesiastical discipline, and on spirituality which is the basis of human existence."

Siri also made the point that John Paul I had "completed his mission." He had done what he had to do. The same note was struck by Cardinal Timothy Manning of Los Angeles: "He made his statement—and then dropped off the stage." There were also hints that Providence had been wise in removing so swiftly someone whose naïveté and ignorance of world affairs had already gotten him into trouble.

Perhaps his worst mistake was to receive General Videla,

president of Argentina, without realizing that this would be badly received by Latin American Catholics who were preparing their Puebla meeting, where they hoped to deliver a salutary shock to military dictators with their theory of the "national security state." On the other hand, Cardinal Joseph Ratzinger, archbishop of Munich, warned the conclave that it would be under intense pressure to go for a candidate who favored an "opening to the left" or the "historic compromise" with the Communists and that this should be resisted. John Paul I had been critical of liberation theology, and that tradition should be continued by the next pope.

On Saturday October 14, 111 cardinals went into the conclave. For the first time in history the number of non-European cardinals (56) exceeded that of Europeans (55). Of the non-Europeans, 19 were Latin Americans, 13 North Americans, 12 Africans, 9 Asians, and 4 from Oceania. There were still 26 Italians. Little is known of the dynamics of this conclave. Certainly there was drama, hinted at in the remark of Cardinal Enrique y Tarancón: "God made use of human malignity and of divisions among the Italians."

Who were the competing Italians who knocked each other out? According to Siri's secretary, "Cardinal Siri lacked only a few votes to obtain the required majority. Not more than four or five."[11] This source, admittedly too close to be entirely reliable, also asserts that Siri would have been pope, had he been willing to envisage Cardinal Giovanni Benelli of Florence as his secretary of state—which he was not prepared to do. The four ballots of the first day did not produce a solution. Siri was the candidate of reaction and Benelli of openness to the world. But though they came close, neither could reach the required majority.

A variety of factors conspired to propel Karol Wojtyla through the gap this left. The first was that the conclave had run out of pastorally minded Italians of sufficient caliber. Therefore there was an opening for a non-Italian. Wyszynski's paper at the August conclave suggested that if a "strong doctrinal pope" were needed, then Eastern Europe could provide one. Moreover, after the death of John Paul I, physical fitness was essential, a young fifty-eight-year-old who skied and climbed mountains would fit the bill. Again, Wojtyla had been elected to the council of the 1971 synod—it had only twelve elected members—and he was very active in promoting its work. Cardinal Sebastiano Baggio, head of the Congregation for Bishops, set him up to give the position papers at the synod of 1974 on evangelization. Wojtyla dealt very satisfactorily in Baggio's view with the drift to liberation theology. Wojtyla was, in fact, better known than Luciani. Was Baggio his *grande elettore*?

There was something very special about this conclave. Something unusual and unprecedented happened. The late Cardinal John J. Carberry, the harmonica-playing archbishop of St. Louis, said, typically, "I would like to tell you everything. It would thrill you. But I can't." Cardinal Siri told Benny Lai that it would be a good thing—some time in the future—to tell how this conclave went, "for secrecy," he said darkly, "though valid at the time of the conclave, can cover over some very uncharitable actions."[12] Karol Wojtyla, after his election, remarked that electing him showed "great courage."

Now, there is a theory that meets these requirements. By Sunday evening, the conclave mood was rather depressed. No one was seriously emerging. They could spend a lot of time trying out candidates who manifestly could not rally the necessary support, but that would mean going around in circles. At this point, Cardinal Franz König of Vienna, supported by Cardinal Joseph Ratzinger (it is alleged), suggested a departure from precedent. Instead of allowing the conclave to be dominated by unavowed "factions" or "parties," could they not try out, as a way of resolving the impasse, a really surprise candidate like Karol Wojtyla? His merits were known. He could bring the vigor of the East to the rather tired West. His Italian was excellent.[13]

Once the idea was proposed, it gained ground rapidly until, by lunchtime the following day, Wojtyla was ahead and by the eighth ballot elected. A kind of confirmation was conveyed by the remark of Cardinal Hyacinthe Thiandoum, archbishop of Dakar, who said, "We were surprised by the emergence of this candidate. If his name had emerged on the first day, everything would have gone more swiftly."

Another detail, from another source, completes the picture. Cardinal Giovanni Colombo, who succeeded Paul VI in Milan and was his confidant, refused to be considered as a candidate. At seventy-six he felt too old (though that was the age of John XXIII when he was elected). He added a "revelation." Paul VI believed that a man of seventy-five would rarely be capable of keeping up with the demands of the modern papacy. He considered resigning himself, but was talked out of it. He did not wish to create a precedent such that every pope, on reaching seventy-five, would *have to* resign. But he wanted the conclave to know his judgment that if a pope felt unable to continue after seventy-five, he should be free to resign without feeling he was setting a precedent.

This remark was made at the August conclave of 1978. But it became more relevant than ever in the October conclave. It meant the cardinals could elect a fifty-eight-year-old pope without committing themselves to an immensely long pontificate. So Cardinal Karol Wojtyla became pope on October 16, 1978. After possibly toying with the name Stanislaus, he opted for the safer course of Pope John Paul II, which the Roman crowd practically imposed on him. His pontificate of surprises began with the biggest surprise of all: his election.

FOUR

John Paul II and His Polish Legacy

So John Paul II was, by a quirk of fate, careful planning by Cardinal Baggio, the intervention of Cardinal König, or the operations of Divine Providence, unexpectedly elected pope on October 16, 1978.

When the cardinals gather at the next conclave in Rome, they will begin with an analysis of how his pontificate has gone. What inheritance will he bequeath to the Church? Judgments on this score are not lacking. "Conservatives" applaud him as the man who restored order and Catholic identity after the (as they see it) confusions and vacillations of Pope Paul VI. "Liberals" deplore him as the man who restored the monarchical papacy, undermined the collegiality of the bishops proclaimed by Vatican II, and while "saving" the Church in central and Eastern Europe, antagonized theologians and risked losing the Church in Latin America by attacking liberation theology. Godlike objectivity is impossible in such matters.

There is a great difficulty in speaking honestly and directly about popes, for as soon as a man becomes pope a process of mythologization sets in that transforms overnight the mediocre into a genius and the merely talented into a superluminary. No one—outside the narrow circle of phenomenologists—had paid much attention to the philosophical work of Karol Wojtyla.

Yet once he became pope, *The Acting Person* was translated into the main European languages; and the Catholic University of Lublin, which had isolated him when he was teaching there, began the intensive study of his works as though he were, as they soon claimed, "one of the greatest thinkers of the twentieth century." Such assertions look patently absurd once the pope is dead, but while he is alive they combine with "creeping infallibility" to make any criticism difficult. The pope, as Vatican I says clearly, is endowed only with "that infallibility with which the Church is endowed" and can exercise his charism of infallibility only in exceptional situations. There has been only one such occasion since 1870: the definition of the Assumption of 1950. But a kind of spectral aura or penumbra of infallibility comes to envelop the pope's every utterance. Pope John Paul has even been heard exhorting the Cagliari soccer team to attend carefully to the (his) ordinary magisterium. To little avail.

The problem is compounded in a pope who has such a clear sense of his providential mission. What is the providential meaning of this controversial pontificate? The cardinals of the college are no better placed than anyone else for making this judgment. But they will at least be able to make their analysis in private, which can add a certain frankness, even though they are nearly all, by now, men appointed by John Paul himself and therefore owing loyalty to him in a special way.

The next conclave will have one feature that no conclave has ever had before: never before has there been a conclave after a *Polish* pope. One sure thing is that another Polish pope will not emerge, not only because none of the Polish cardinals have enough stature, but because it would suggest a Polish takeover. One Polish pope is quite enough for a century or so. A Roman joke says that the mysterious third secret of Fátima is "Repent and pray— or you will have another Polish pope." So one aspect of the analysis of the pontificate will be to determine what Polish features it possesses, for they will obviously not be repeatable.

So the old question asked on the eve of every conclave—continuity or discontinuity?—will be asked in a new form. The difficulty lies in sorting out what is particularly Polish from what is generally conservative. For example, is Pope John Paul's partiality for Opus Dei to be attributed to his Polishness or his conservatism? There can be no doubt about the fact of his partiality. The contrast is very marked between his attitude toward Opus Dei and that toward the great religious orders like the Jesuits, the Dominicans, and the Franciscans, all of whom have been shabbily treated. His affection for Opus Dei was strong enough for him to allow the beatification of Josemaría Escrivá to go ahead despite well-founded protests and obvious irregularities. Was that part of being Polish or being conservative?

In a rare interview in late 1993 Pope John Paul was asked by Jas Gawronski what difference being Polish made to his pontificate. The second part of his answer was rather surprising:

> *I grew up there, and therefore have brought with me the history, the culture, the experience and the language of Poland. Even now when I write something, I write it in Polish.*

Having lived in a country which had to struggle for its freedom, in a country vulnerable to the aggression and dictates of its neighbors, I have been led to sympathize with the plight of the countries of the Third World, which also are subject to another type of dependence, the economic one. . . . I have understood what exploitation is, and I have sided unequivocally with the poor, with the disinherited, the oppressed, the marginalized and the defenseless.[1]

Yet John Paul's way of siding with the poor has not been in the manner of those in the Third World who have inserted themselves at their side. He has issued social encyclicals, like the 1987 *Sollicitudo Rei Socialis,* that reaffirm again and again the Church's "love of preference for the poor"—it means the same as the "option for the poor," but does not have the same associations with liberation theology. But the changes made in Church practice in Latin America have brought the Church back from much of its social involvement to concentrate more on the spiritual life. This is love of the poor with a Polish slant, discouraged by the fear of Communism from working too hard at material changes.

One of the key moments in John Paul's pontificate came on his return to Poland in June 1979, within a year of his election. The first non-Italian pope in 455 years happened to be a Slav. When he met Mikhail Gorbachev in December 1991, the Soviet president congratulated him on being the first Polish pope. John Paul gently corrected him: "The first Slav Pope." "But you are a West Slav," said Gorbachev. "It is the same," said John Paul, thus casting his spell over Gorbachev and drawing him within his pastoral orbit. If there really was a "common European home," as Gorbachev had announced in Prague in 1987, then only the pope could welcome him into it.

But that was "future music" when Pope John Paul stood

before a million well-disciplined and orderly people in Victory Square, Warsaw, on Saturday, June 2, 1979, the eve of Pentecost. It was an extraordinary event. In the heart of a Communist capital, Warsaw—a stone's throw away from the tomb of the Polish unknown soldier, whose battles began in the Middle Ages—a huge cross was erected. It was dismantled before sunset that same day.

The pope ended his homily with the words: "Come Holy Spirit, fill the hearts of the faithful and renew the face of the earth." But then he added, with a sweeping gesture, "of this earth." The Polish word for "earth" *(ziemen)* also means "land" or "country." In other words he was beseeching the Holy Spirit to liberate Poland. This was no mere rhetorical flourish.

No pope has thought more, or at any rate written more, about Europe than John Paul II. It would not be unreasonable to speak of an obsession with Europe. But his image of Europe, his *Europabild,* is not one to which most of us are accustomed. It is in some ways rather disconcerting. It is always Europe seen from Poland.

His first major address on Europe came from Gniezno, the Canterbury of Poland, where the earliest Polish kings are buried and which boasts the shrine of St. Adalbert. Here occurred in 966 the founding act of the Polish Church: the baptism of Miesko I. History for John Paul is a storehouse of powerful images. Every May 3 he went to Gniezno for the feast of St. Adalbert, which is also known as Constitution Day after the first Polish constitution of 1791.

The point was crystal clear. In Poland no wedge can be driven between conversion to Christianity and the establishment of the nation: they were one and the same event. *Chrzest,* the Polish word for "baptism," is more like our word "christen." This is why the pope so often uses formulas like "France, remember your baptism" and why "de-Christianization" for him represents apostasy. In Poland in 1979 he proclaimed the "spiritual unity" of Europe at a time when the continent was still physically divided by the Iron Curtain. He declared, in effect, the division of Europe anomalous and its frontiers irrelevant. In Poland he acted as a "tribune of the people," articulating what was felt but could not be said. That gave the Polish workers enough self-confidence to found Solidarity. But Poland's "vocation" depended on the "founding act" of 966.

John Paul applies this notion elsewhere. He saw Columbus's "discovery" of America in 1492 as another founding act, the beginning of evangelization and civilization, interchangeable terms. Within that framework are other "founding acts," such as the moment when the cross was planted on the shore of Vera Cruz and Brazil came into existence on May 3, 1500, feast of the Holy Cross. But it is in Europe that the founding act of baptism is seen most vividly and has evident political implications.

The baptism of Rus in the land of Kiev in 988 was the theme of two encyclicals on its millennium. John Paul said: "We unite ourselves with all those who recognize in the baptism received by their ancestors the source of their religious, cultural and national identity."[2] This was clearly an attempt to stake a claim on the Russian Orthodox tradition, in his view equally well represented by the Ukrainian Catholic Church (or Uniate Church). Of Lithuania he said: "Christianity was the true evangelical leaven of the nation, it marked its daily life, it put down solid roots and so became, so to speak, its soul." Always there is this triad of religion-culture-nature, which are seen as inseparable.

There was another aspect of John Paul's Gniezno address in 1979. These were early days in which he pinched himself and asked why he was elected pope. What was the providential meaning of his pontificate? What was God trying to say through his election?

Most of us would be loathe to answer such a question very precisely—who can scrutinize the ways of the Lord? But John Paul's answer was very clear. He had been chosen as pope to bring to the whole Church community the special contribution of the Slavic peoples to Europe in particular:

> *Does not Christ wish to hear . . . with special understanding, special sensitivity, those sounds of human speech which are interlinked in a common root, a common etymology and which . . . sound so close to each other? Is not the Holy Spirit disposed to see that this Polish Pope, this Slav Pope, should at this very moment reveal the spiritual unity of Europe?*[3]

This hint at the providential meaning of his election was couched in the form of rhetorical questions, but that modesty takes away none of its force.

So in Gniezno John Paul was not just the heir of the Polish national tradition, with its religious and cultural dimensions. From there he proclaimed the "spiritual unity of Europe" not as some kind of task to be realized, but as an already accomplished fact. Europe, still in 1979 manifestly divided by the Iron Curtain, by ideological opposition, and by threatening military alliances, was "spiritually united." Did this mean united in the mind? Was the spiritual unity of Europe just "something that goes on in the head"? Was it the kind of "idealism" for which Marxists habitually had such contempt?

For the pope, the word *spiritual*, far from meaning unreal, means what is most really real. Compared with the centuries of shared European history, the forty or so years since Yalta divided Europe were a mere blink, a temporary aberration. So it followed that the divisions of Europe were humanly created, artificial, and therefore doomed. It is easy enough to see that now, and even to regard it as a truism, but in 1979 it was a bold and very challenging claim.

If one asked in 1979 just what was being united, the pope's answer would be peoples first and then, perhaps, nations. He needed this distinction, because throughout the nineteenth century Poland was carved up between its three powerful neighbors, Austria, Prussia, and Russia. His father, he pointed out, was no less Polish for having an Austrian passport and serving in the Austro-Hungarian army. But to be spiritually united means nothing unless there are real exchanges. Though the frontiers of Europe could not be totally ignored in the 1980s, they were increasingly disregarded or regarded as anomalous, so much so that when they crumbled late in 1989, people wondered why the dogs, mines, trip wires, and border shootings had ever existed.

John Paul's image of Europe included a vision—there is no other word for it—of a Europe without frontiers through which people wander freely. But they wander purposefully. They go on pilgrimages. For the pope the key pilgrimage center that forged European awareness was Santiago de Compostela, where the remains of St. James are located. Here is what he said about it in autumn 1982:

> In the centuries when a homogeneous and spiritually united continent was being shaped, the whole of Europe came here to the "memorial" of St. James. It was one of the places that favored the mutual understanding of the so very different European peoples, the Latins, the Germans, the Celts, the Anglo-Saxons and the Slavs. The pilgrimage brought together, put in contact and united all those peoples who throughout the centuries, once touched by the preaching of Christ's apostles, accepted the Gospel, and at the same time were born as peoples and nations.[4]

So it is not just the nations, it is Europe itself that is baptized and acquires its identity through its baptism.

Now this is a highly sacralized view of the continent. The pope's map of Europe is very special and selective. It does not include steelworks or power stations or computer-based industries; it marks Marian pilgrimage centers like Czestochowa, Velherad, Lourdes, and Knock and shrines connected with local saints. This sacred Euro-map is superimposed upon the ordinary map. Everything that is not directly linked to the fundamental vision is omitted.

Protestants like Luther and Calvin are excluded. Even the Catholic Erasmus did not rate a mention on the visit to the Netherlands. If these fellow Christians cannot edge their way in, then there is no hope at all for the secular thinkers who have made their mark on Europe. It is true that John Paul did mention Goethe at Compostela, but only to say that Goethe suggested that "European awareness" was born on pilgrimage. Secular thinkers are allowed to reinforce, but not to challenge, the main vision.

This sacralized Europe cuts clean across the ordinary perception of Europe as to some extent post-Christian. John Paul's vision does not fit the realities of the Europe we actually experience. He cheerfully accepts that his message challenges the conventional wisdom, is a sign of contradiction (the title of one of his books), and flings down the gauntlet to contemporary Europe. He does not mind that at all. He loves a scrap.

Perhaps the reason he prefers Compostela to Rome itself is that it developed as the Moors—the Muslims—had been driven out of Spain. It fits the crusading spirit better. Its intellectual world is that of the first European epic, the *Song of Roland,* in which *"Chrestiens unt raison, païens unt tort"* ("the Christians are right, and the pagans are wrong"). The solemn rhetoric of Compostela is all devoted to a rediscovery. The *re-* prefixes abound: "I, bishop of Rome and pastor of the universal Church, from St. James of Compostela, send my cry of love toward you, old Europe. Rediscover yourself, be yourself. Revivify your roots. Relive the authentic values that have been the glory of your history." Is it a restoration he has in mind? Does he dream of a new Christendom in which there would be an overlap, a perfect fit, between religious and social life? He hasn't used the term, and it seems an impossible dream.

Yet something analogous is implied by all the talk of a "second evangelization" of Europe, which has been such a feature of the pontificate. It is addressed to the young in particular. He appealed to them in Ravenna in 1986 "to bring about a second evangelization of European society by your effective commitment. That's a task that belongs to young people especially and challenges them. The 'refoundation' of European culture is the most decisive and urgent enterprise of our time."[5] This project, whatever it really means, is concerned with European *society*.

There is in the pope no privatization of Christian faith, hope, or charity. He wants them all to be embodied in the structures of society, and this is the primary task of laypeople. But the reverse of this particular medal is that making an impact on society also means refusing the distinction between law and morality. It means in practice that the pope has no use for pluralism and that he would ideally like legislation to reflect Catholic moral teaching whether Catholics are in a majority or not. So "bringing the second evangelization to European society" really means mobilizing people, especially young people, for a series of moral campaigns.

Equipped with this image of Europe, Pope John Paul has never liked the way the European Union (né Community) made off with the adjective *European*. Neither the European Commission nor the European Parliament, to which it is supposedly accountable, display a broad enough concept of Europe for him. Their attempts, after Maastricht, to conduct a coherent foreign policy seem to him derisory: Europe's sad incapacity to put a stop to the tragedy of the former Yugoslavia suggests that he is not wholly wrong.

There is a paradox here. John Paul's Europe is a Europe of peoples, of nations, and it stretches like Charles de Gaulle's Europe from the Atlantic to the Urals. He attaches so much importance to the baptism of Rus, because it permits him to get, roughly, to the Urals, for that marks the easternmost point of penetration of Christianity into Asia. John Paul counts Russia conditionally as part of "our common European home." In the last article he wrote before becoming pope, he inquired where the easternmost border of Europe was to be found. It was not on any map: it occurred where the Christian emphasis on the dignity of the individual human person met the enslavement and tyranny that came from the East.

So one of John Paul's first acts as pope was to proclaim Sts. Cyril and Methodius coequal patrons of Europe alongside St. Benedict. Paul VI had declared Benedict patron of Europe in 1964. Benedictine monasticism is fine, but it is too closely associated with Western Europe. By setting the two brothers from Salonika and apostles of the Slavs alongside St. Benedict of Nursia, John Paul was correcting what he saw as a historic imbalance between West and East. He was trying to right a profound historical injustice. Poles resented the fact that the Eastern, and specifically the Slavic, contribution to the universal Church had not been properly recognized. Poles had been smarting for a long time under their inability to make themselves understood. Cyril and Methodius represent the "wider Europe" before the divisions of East and West occurred. They are presented as precursors of ecumenism and models of evangelization today, since they translated the Gospels into the language of the Slavic peoples. *Slavorum Apostoli* was the first encyclical devoted to Europe.

Moreover, and this is another constant theme, the Church needs both traditions just as the body needs two lungs to breathe—the "Latin" tradition, which is rational, juridical, and practical, needs filling out by the Oriental tradition, which is more mystical, intuitive, and charismatic (in the sense of led by the Holy Spirit).

The greater part of the magisterium of Pope John Paul can be read as a way of trying to bring to the West this wisdom of the East. For example, the encyclical on suffering, *Salvifici Doloris* (February 11, 1984), is a reproach to Western superficiality for failing to grapple with the reality of evil in a century that has known "an incomparable accumulation of sufferings, even to the possible self-destruction of the planet" (p. 8). In this dramatic and apocalyptic view, to be talking about birth control or women priests seems intolerably shallow.

Western Europeans are accustomed to thinking of themselves as on center stage, no doubt presumptuously. John Paul simply moved the center stage eastward to Warsaw. In June 1987 he stood before the Palace of Culture in Warsaw, that embarrassing building that Stalin gave as a "gift" to the people of Warsaw. (He made them pay for it, and it is now, ironically enough, the stock exchange.) Looking eastward with his back to the building, John Paul sketched out his vision of the universal Church: "The Church which is in Lithuania, Belorussia, in Ukraine, in Kiev and in the territories of Great Russia and of our brother Slavs (and also the non-Slavs), to the south in the countries once visited by the saintly brothers Cyril and Methodius." This is what happens when you look eastward, with a side glance at the Balkans. The rest of the map was quickly filled in: "And in all of Europe. In the American continents that are preparing to celebrate the 500th anniversary of their evangelization. In Africa, Australia and Asia, and in all the islands and archipelagoes of all the seas and oceans." It is always chastening to be put firmly in one's place, and a new experience for Western Europeans to be relegated to "the rest of Europe."

In this picture of the world, Western Europe stands behind the pope, at his shoulders as it were, and that is why it needs its "second evangelization." It has to be disciplined and well ordered, marshaled and in line. The appointments of conservative bishops and the curbs on theologians are seen as part of this process: it is a matter of getting the troops in line.

Such thoughts are not just an exhortation for internal Church use—still less, pulpit rhetoric. When he had an opportunity in October 1988 to address the most representative elected body in Europe, the European Parliament, John Paul did not change or adapt his language to the circumstances. Far from it, he struck a blow at the very basis of its tolerance of pluralism. When, he said, all subordination of the creature to God and all reference to a transcendent order of truth and goodness are excluded, the human is made the measure of all things. What happens then? "Ethics then has no foundation other than social consensus and individual liberty has no brake other than what society thinks it must impose for the safeguard of others."[6] That describes the practical, workaday ethics on which pluralist societies like ours do in fact have to operate.

In Strasbourg the pope warned about the "somber perspectives" that would open up for all Europeans if God were eased out of public life. Why is this so dangerous? Because the "supreme guarantee against all abuses of power by man over man" would no longer be available. It is very attractive to think of God as saving us from the idolatry of the state or a dictator like Stalin, and that is part of Pope John Paul's own Polish experience. But it is possible to think that the separation of powers between the executive, the legislative, and the judiciary is another more earthbound guarantee against tyranny that can also come in useful. But the pope did not present his views as something to be debated. He was Cassandra, warning of catastrophe.

John Paul's anticommunist crusade succeeded. Beyond his dreams. Beyond anyone's dreams. The encyclical *Centesimus Annus*, published in 1991 on the hundredth anniversary of Leo XIII's social encyclical *Rerum Novarum*, celebrated this victory. It included a paean to democracy such as had not been seen before: "The Church values the democratic system inasmuch as it ensures the participation of citizens in making political choices, guarantees to the governed the possibility both of electing and holding accountable those who govern them, and of replacing them through peaceful means where appropriate" (p. 46). This reflected the Polish experience, in which democracy appeared as the only peaceable alternative to totalitarian rule. But if the dramatic liberation from Communism was, as Cardinal Józef Glemp said, like the crossing of the Red Sea by the people of Israel, since then there has been much floundering about in the desert, cries for more manna, and murmurings against Moses. Does this mean that the commitment to democracy has been weakened?

Yes and no. There is a nuance. In his encyclical *Veritatis Splendor*, Pope John Paul warns against "the risk of an alliance between democracy and ethical relativism, which would remove any sure moral reference points from political and social life" (101). He then quotes another passage from *Centesimus Annus* that was overlooked in the residual euphoria of 1991: "As history demonstrates, a democracy without values easily turns into open or thinly disguised totalitarianism." If the pope is right in seeing a link between "democracy and ethical relativism," then the outlook for democracy in Africa and Eastern Europe is bleak and the position of Catholics in pluralist democracies is put in jeopardy. The pope is tempted by theocracy.

The late Jerzy Turowicz, former editor of *Tygodnik Powszechny*, the Kraków Catholic weekly, knew the pope as a friend since 1949 and was a lucid and courageous man. In 1990 he wrote an editorial entitled "Where We Come from and Where We Are Going," in which he says:

> There are people who think that totalitarianism in the service of a false ideology is wrong, whereas when in the service of a correct and true ideology it is good. That is false. Catholicism (and Christianity too) is not an ideology, and every totalitarianism is wrong. . . . The state is the common property of all citizens, irrespective of their confession, nationality or convictions. Poland is not the exclusive property of Catholics, no matter how numerous they may be. The slogan "To be Polish is to be Catholic" has a good meaning when it indicates the bond of this nation with the faith of the Church. But it is bad when it serves to divide people or treat people of other confessions or unbelievers as second-class citizens. . . . Catholics do not have the right to compel others to accept their convictions.[7]

Pope John Paul's Polish perspective gave him a particular awareness of the need to make amends in the Church's relationship with one group it has treated as second-class citizens, the Jews. No doubt the presence of Auschwitz on Polish soil made him particularly sensitive on this issue. Thomas Keneally's novel *Schindler's Ark* (*Schindler's List* in the Spielberg film version) recalls the wartime Kraków he knew so well.

In *Nostra Aetate* the Second Vatican Council rejected anti-Semitism and exculpated the Jews from "deicide." But John Paul has gone much further than any of his predecessors in providing the basis for a new understanding between Christians and Jews. He was the first pope ever to visit the Rome synagogue—there has been a synagogue in Rome since the time of Christ—where he declared in 1986 that the Jewish people were our "elder brothers."

In December 1993, the Fundamental Agreement between the Holy See and Israel was signed. This paved the way for diplomatic relations—their absence had been a matter for long-standing complaint. On April 7, 1994, the pope was joined by some Auschwitz survivors for a concert with works by Leonard Bernstein performed by the London Royal Philharmonic Orchestra.

Then on March 16, 1998, the Vatican released a document, "We Remember: A Reflection on the Shoah," intended as an apology to the Jews in preparation for the jubilee year 2000. Though it had taken eleven years to prepare, it disappointed the Jews, because there was no admission that the Church as such had ever borne responsibility for fostering anti-Jewish prejudices, but only that there had been errors and failures on the part of some Christians. Still, it represented a half successful attempt to open up a new era in Christian-Jewish relations. The next pope will not go back on that.

However, everything so far said in this chapter will appear unbearably Eurocentric to some Asians, Latin Americans, and Africans. They will be disappointed to learn that "liberalism" has replaced "Communism" as the target of the pope's crusade. The whole discussion remains locked in a time warp in which the most important events are the Reformation and the eighteenth-century Enlightenment. For non-Europeans (and for Europeans too, did they but know it), the North-South divide has replaced the East-West preoccupation; and the North is rich and well fed, while the South is poor and hungry.

This is the most important challenge to be faced by the world, and consequently the Church, at the end of the twentieth century. The world today is often pictured as a champagne glass, a wide, shallow bowl atop a slender stem. The billion people who live in the industrialized nations are the "champagne" people, less than a fifth of the world's population yet with more than four-fifths of the world's income. In this perspective the spread of democracy in recent years, though welcome, leaves untouched the realm of poverty, where access to the ordinary opportunities of life—land, water, work, living space, and basic social services—is all the time shrinking. Hence the conclusion of the 1992 *Human Development Report:* "Some people claim that recent events prove the triumph of capitalism and the demise of socialism. This is too simplistic a view. If there is a triumph of capitalism, it need not be a triumph of greed. If there is a demise of socialism, it need not be the demise of all social objectives." This is not so very different from what Pope John Paul himself said in Riga, addressing Latvian intellectuals. But he did not put it in a North-South context.

The next pontificate will see the world in those terms. From this point of view, the pontificate of Pope John Paul II will appear to history as a Polish interlude. It is exciting, heroic, and exceptional (in the sense of an *état d'exception*), and after it a more mundane and feet-on-the-ground papacy will be desirable.

I know it is a myth, but the image that springs to mind is of the chivalrous Polish knight on a white charger who fearlessly tackles the panzers of the modern world and perishes in the attempt to reverse the secular course of European history. But if it is a failure, it is a noble and heroic one, grandiose in its scope and aims.

Pope John Paul II in 1993 at Mile High Stadium in
Denver, Colorado, during World Youth Day celebrations.

ABOVE: Cardinals gathered in the Sistine Chapel, October 14, 1978, before the conclave that elected Pope John Paul II.

RIGHT: Ballots were burned in this small stove at the conclave that elected Pope John XXIII in 1958.

TOP: Cardinal Carlo Martini, Cardinal Francis Arinze
BOTTOM: Cardinal Christoph Schönborn, Cardinal Giacomo Biffi

TOP: Cardinal Thomas Winning, Cardinal Roger Mahony
BOTTOM: Cardinal Jean-Claude Turcotte, Cardinal Joseph Ratzinger

TOP: Cardinal Juan Sandoval Iñiguez,
Cardinal Darío Castrillón Hoyos
BOTTOM: Cardinal Jan Schotte, Cardinal Achille Silvestrini

TOP: Cardinal Camillo Ruini, Cardinal Lucas Moreira Neves
BOTTOM: Cardinal Edward Cassidy, Cardinal Pio Laghi

TOP: Bishop Francois Xavier Nguyen Van Thuan,
Cardinal Dionigi Tettamanzi
BOTTOM: Cardinal Alfonso López Trujillo,
Cardinal Jorge Arturo Medina Estévez

FIVE John Paul II and Vatican II

The Polish perspective on Europe and the world is the main key that unlocks the meaning of Pope John Paul II's pontificate. But it is not the only one. The Second Vatican Council (1962–65) remains the most epoch-making event in the life of the Catholic Church in the twentieth century. The pontificate of Paul VI was a conscious attempt to implement Vatican II and to bring out the "spiritual dialectic" that underpinned it. The question naturally arises: What was Pope John Paul's attitude toward Vatican II?

On his election he declared that the full implementation of Vatican II would be the program of his pontificate. Was that really true? Before the conclave begins, during the *Novemdiales,* the conclave will have to decide how the pontificate that just ended really stands in regard to Vatican II. It will not regard lip service as sufficient.

"Actions speak louder than words" can be applied to John Paul's pontificate. Though Paul VI has been lavishly praised as "our venerable predecessor," he is presented as a tragic figure who couldn't quite cope. John Paul's actions say clearly that he considers Paul VI to have been weak and vacillating, if not utterly mistaken, on priestly identity, religious life, dangerous theologians, episcopal collegiality, ecumenism, and Vatican II itself. In his judgment Paul VI was too lenient in his treatment of allegedly dissident theologians, did not push hard enough on *Humanae. Vitae*, surrendered Catholic identity in his ecumenical enthusiasm, and failed to show sufficient firmness in dealing with the Jesuits and other religious orders, especially women's religious orders already "infected" with feminism.

The Extraordinary Synod of 1985, with its abandonment of "the People of God" as the key concept for the understanding of the Church and its "pessimistic" reediting of the "signs of the times," confirmed that Paul VI's interpretation of Vatican II was being rejected. This is grave, because Paul VI's interpretation of Vatican II was the standard view shared by bishops, priests, theologians, and Christians generally.

There is a paradox here. No doubt John Paul II was sincere in his proclamations of fidelity to Vatican II, but he was committed to Vatican II as interpreted in a highly idiosyncratic way. This is another instance of the highly personal nature of this pontificate.

While theologians in the West were interpreting the council as an innovation, Karol Wojtyla saw it as an unruffled reinforcement of traditional views. It did not generate excitement about change or involve new participation of the laity or any great hope for the renewal of the Church. He saw it as a confirmation of the Church in the way it was going. So there was a basic misunderstanding between Poland and the rest of the developed world on what the council really meant.

The failed assassination attempt in 1981 confirmed John Paul in his personal approach to the pontificate. Some might call it a messianistic approach. He certainly feels that, having Providence on his side, he has something to teach the whole Church. The principal effect was that he no longer needed to listen to any advice within the Church and could concentrate on his personal agenda. Time and time again, he warned that "the Church is not a democracy" and castigated the abusive exploitation of the idea of the Church as "the People of God." But perhaps the most important lesson of the failed attempt was the extraordinary forgiveness that John Paul extended from the start to his would-be assassin. Four days after the shooting he was broadcasting from his hospital bed in a very shaky voice, saying, "With deep emotion I pray for that brother who shot me and whom I have sincerely forgiven," and a couple of years later he went to visit him in prison.

One major innovation of his papacy, which he saw very much as an implementation of the council, was his program of papal journeys. Though Paul VI had visited the Holy Land, the United Nations, and India, John Paul II seems to have penetrated every corner of the globe. By the end of 1999 he had made 89 journeys to 117 nations. His visit to Poland in June 1979 was only the first of 8 to his native land, and he kept up the fierce pace to the end. One of the most successful was Cuba in January 1998, where Fidel Castro welcomed him with unfeigned warmth and respect. What has this to do with Vatican II? It is one form of bringing the Church into the modern world, one way of highlighting the world community and the solidarity between nations. But on the other hand, it shifts the emphasis from the Bishop of Rome to the Pastor of the Universal Church. So while it increases the communication between the pope and the college of bishops, it also reaffirms his control over them. No other pope will be able to compete with John Paul II in jetting around the globe, and it would be a mistake to try to emulate his energy—not to mention the expense involved. A precedent has been set, however, that it will not be easy to ignore.

Although the journeys have been the most striking innovation of this pontificate, there have also been other major achievements. In 1983 John Paul II promulgated the new Code of Canon Law. In 1991, in the First European Synod, he welcomed the collapse of Communism, to which he had undoubtedly contributed importantly. The next year, 1992, saw the publication of *The Catechism of the Catholic Church* in Italy and France. It came out in Britain and the United States in mid-1994, after translation difficulties about "inclusive language."

But the longer this papacy continues and the more attempts there are to call the Church to order, the greater the despair that the legacy of Vatican II is being washed away. There is a widespread feeling of malaise: the pontificate is malfunctioning. For all the intense and incessant activity, the voluminous flow of encyclicals and instructions, the endless globe-trotting, the pontificate is to some extent whirling away in a void, cut off from the real life of the People of God. The disappointing answer to the question, What more is there for this pontificate to do? is, Yet more of the same.

When Pope John Paul is accused of overriding the wishes of the People of God, he always replies that the Church is not a democracy and truth is not created by a show of hands. But, as the prophetic figure of Pedro Casaldáliga, bishop of São Félix, Brazil, remarked: "The Church is not a democracy, sure. I don't want the Church to be a democracy. I want it to be something better than a democracy. I want it to be a community." A prophet speaking. Casaldáliga was reproached for not going on *ad limina* visits to the pope that bishops must make every five years. Finally, after seventeen years, he made it to Rome in 1988. He was interrogated about his views on liberation theology by Cardinal Bernardin Gantin. "You said that *ad limina* visits were useless," Gantin complained. Casaldáliga corrected him: "Almost useless."

When he got to see Pope John Paul—for fifteen minutes—they discussed a future visit to Brazil. Casaldáliga suggested that Gantin's desire to have his replies in writing suggested a lack of trust. "It can also be a sign of confidence," John Paul replied. "Cardinal Paulo Evaristo Arns, when he comes here likes to have things in writing." Then the pope sat down, opened his arms, and, "half-jesting and half-warning," explained, "So that you may see I am no wild beast." Casaldáliga did not know what to make of this.

But he was right in thinking that the truism that "the Church is not a democracy" was used to eliminate not only all dissent, but all serious consultation in the Church. All the organs of consultation set in place by Vatican II were one by one emasculated. The Synod of Bishops, which was intended to continue the collegiality, or team spirit, between all the world's bishops, was turned into a rally supporting the papal theses. A high point of futility was reached at the 1990 Synod on the Role of the Priest when the notion of ordaining married men because of acute pastoral need was rejected out of hand. Presented as a free "decision" of the synod, it was imposed on the synod by papal *fiat*. Undeterred, the Oceanian bishops made another bid for the ordination of married catechists in the November 1998 synod, when four out of the six discussion groups raised the issue in their group reports. But everyone knew that nothing would happen.

The devaluation of the synod was only one aspect of the general undermining of episcopal or collegial authority. A study was ordered, allegedly in response to the 1985 Synod on Vatican II (Extraordinary Synod), on the exact theological status and nature of episcopal conferences (or local benches of bishops). When John Paul eventually published his apostolic letter, *Apostolos Suos,* in August 1998, he denied episcopal conferences any theological or collegial reality, leaving all authority to teach in the hands either of individual bishops, on the one hand, or of the universal college of bishops, on the other. So when bishops enter the episcopal conference, they leave their authority outside with their umbrellas and coats in the cloakroom. But when episcopal authority is thus undermined, then *a fortiori* the laity are reduced to complete passivity, growling impotence, and silent fury.

In the way he has centered authority around himself, Pope John Paul II seems utterly unaware of what he has done to the credibility of the Church. He cannot grasp the truth contained in the bitter criticism of Oxford zoologist Richard Dawkins, a professional anti-Christian: "Pope John Paul II is a courageous man of rocklike character. . . . He heroically epitomizes the preposterous institution of which he is head. He is perfectly poised to do it the greatest possible damage and is in the strongest strategic position to do so. Long may he live."[1] The irony is that Pope John Paul's intransigence supplies weapons to the enemies of the Church—the very people whom he wishes to confute.

In an exchange of letters in the *Spectator,* someone defended John Paul and *Veritatis Splendor* on the grounds that he had been professor of ethics in the Catholic University of Lublin. This brought Dawkins sneering out of New College, Oxford, once again:

> *This is no ordinary professor whose views on ethics can be accepted or rejected on his arguments. This professor wouldn't recognize an argument if it bit him. It has been internally revealed to him that he is right, and he has lately reaffirmed his infallibility and he expects—with good reason—that many millions of the poorest and most overcrowded people in the*

world will obey him without question whatever he says. Despite appearances, this is not a gentle smiling old duffer with a harmless penchant for kissing airport taxiways, but a dangerous world-damaging dictator.[2]

This farrago of nonsense—there was no question of infallibility in *Veritatis Splendor*—from the man whom Paul Johnson called "the poor man's Huxley" is here to illustrate that authoritarian teaching does not impress the modern world.

John Paul is not the first pope to have ruled the Church from the extreme right—Pope St. Pius X did the same—but John Paul's historic importance is that he is the first post–Vatican II pope to attempt this tour de force. The natural place for popes is in the middle of the ecclesial road. They must not allow their personal theological opinions to influence their judgments. Otherwise they put the unity of the Church in jeopardy. They must not define the Church too narrowly. John Paul breaks all these rules. As the late John M. Todd, English Catholic layman and founder of the publishing house of Darton, Longman and Todd, perceptively observed, "If Paul VI was a consensus man who won some battles, lost some, and said publicly that he didn't know what to do about others, John Paul II finds decision-making as easy as Paul VI found it difficult."[3] Todd remarked that John Paul's courage, intelligence, and sincerity were not in doubt. Yet each time he seeks to address the modern world or his critics within the Church, he fails. Todd said: "He merely presents one side of the argument, whether he is addressing American Bishops and nuns, the Anglican Church, the married laity, world demographers of the population explosion or others."

This, in the end, will prove to have been the Achilles' heel, or greatest weakness, of the pontificate. To produce one side of the argument is not good enough. It makes the message of the Church unnecessarily incredible. Pope John Paul II is a convictions pope in the sense that Margaret Thatcher was a convictions politician. As with her, you were either "one of us" or "not one of us."

To put it another way, John Paul II does not understand, appreciate, or allow for the existence of a "loyal opposition" in the Church. Because of that, he spurns the simple task of explaining to people why what he said was right. He prefers to crush them by disciplinary measures. He makes the fatal mistake of assuming that "disagreement" meant "dissidence." This "loyal opposition" will emerge in the next conclave.

John Todd remarked on the way Mikhail Gorbachev was impressed, when he met Pope John Paul in December 1989, by the similarities between the Vatican and the Kremlin: a mass of churches and secular buildings crammed within the narrow compass of a walled city-state. The Kremlin, or rather the Soviet system, collapsed because its people ceased to believe in it and because the economy failed to deliver. But that is not the Vatican's situation. Todd said, "Most of the Vatican's critics declare themselves passionate believers in Christianity and supporters of the Catholic tradition; and the economic structure of the Catholic Church, while having taken some knocks, for instance in the banking scandals in which the Vatican was involved, is still viable."

The Vatican is not going to go broke, if the Church bestirs itself. The gates of hell will not prevail against it, and it will survive. But what exactly does that promise mean? One can ask whether it means that the Church will triumph temporally in this world or be enabled to withstand persecution.

But then an even more redoubtable question has to be faced: what was the providential meaning of this controversial pontificate? This is not a question a historian or observer can tackle with any confidence. But one might say that this pontificate has demonstrated, beyond doubt, that a tough-minded, hard-nosed authoritarian papacy cannot commend itself to the modern world. The conservative option has been tried. It has failed. It is time for something different.

Just occasionally, the criticisms that are loud and frequent from independent dissident groups or publications can also be heard from a bishop. Here is Bishop Norbert Werbs from the Hamburg archdiocese speaking up at the First European Synod of bishops meeting in Rome in 1991. Admittedly he is only an auxiliary bishop—and after this he will no doubt remain so—and he is a product of the system he deplores. Yet he found the courage to say in the pope's presence:

1. The peoples of Europe think and feel in an increasingly democratic way. Yet our Church is hierarchically structured. We are convinced that this cannot be given up. Yet we must ask ourselves whether the hierarchical setup of the Church makes possible participation and co-responsibility of all the members of the Church. The consultation process begun by Vatican II seems to many Catholics insufficient. Are they wrong? How could this be improved?

2. In stressing the priesthood of all believers, Vatican II brought out their responsibility for the life of the Church. But many Catholics feel that they are denied any influence in the important process by which bishops are named. They well understand that the bishop must be in communion with the pope. But they cannot understand many recent episcopal appointments. Does this have to be so? How could it be improved?

The question of the appointment of bishops has been one of the most serious areas in which the conciliar awareness of the dignity of the People of God has been violated, and it is one of the areas where the most long-term damage has been done. Whatever the policies of the next pope, he will not be able to change his bishops until, one by one, they reach retirement age. The oversight of the local Church that has been changed for the worse over a time scale of more than twenty years by John Paul II will require just as long a period to be changed back again. Bishops have been parachuted down on dioceses about which they know nothing and where they are doomed to unpopularity.

Thus Joachim Meisner was transferred from East Berlin to Cologne in December 1988. The fact that none of the 815 priests of the diocese of Cologne was deemed capable of becoming bishop and none of the existing West German bishops was thought worthy of promotion seemed like a judgment on the local Church. It required an "outsider" with no experience of life in the West to rule the richest and most prestigious diocese in Germany. Moreover, the provisions of the concordat were arbitrarily set aside.

In the papal mind, these unpopular bishops were meant to "restore order" and impose discipline, often with the aid of Opus Dei. The appointment of Wolfgang Haas to the diocese of Chur in Switzerland represented the most extreme example. Swiss bishops are usually appointed by cathedral chapter election. In this case, the election was avoided by making Haas coadjutor with right of succession in March 1988, a couple of months before his predecessor retired. This was arguably unconstitutional in Swiss law and the agreements signed with the Holy See. Guests at Haas's episcopal consecration, including the prince and princess of Liechtenstein, had to step over the bodies of protesters to make their way into the cathedral.

Haas's appointment was both an *impasse* and a *reductio ad absurdum:* the irresistible force of public opinion met an immovable obstacle—the papal determination to impose this wholly unsuitable man on Chur. By 1993 Haas had been such a disaster as bishop—causing his diocesan pastoral council to dissolve itself in protest at his authoritarian style—that two auxiliaries were appointed to enable the work of the diocese could continue. But even this did not work, and the Swiss bishops' conference demanded "a change in personnel." Eventually in 1997 a new archdiocese of Vaduz was created for Haas by removing the tiny state of Liechtenstein from the old diocese of Chur. Though it comprises only one twenty-seventh part of the original diocese, its classification as an archdiocese enabled Haas's move to be presented as a promotion.

While Chur was struggling with its conservative Bishop Haas, the diocese of Evreux in France was being deprived of its progressive Bishop Jacques Gaillot. This small, serene man, at the same time holy in his manner and challenging in his positions, was relieved of his diocese and retired off at the age of a mere sixty. It was not the first attempt to remove a bishop. Raymond Hunthausen of Seattle, Washington, who took a sympathetic pastoral line on marriage and homosexuality questions, was removed for a time from the effective control of his diocese in 1986, but with Gaillot the move was more drastic and permanent. It was the first time a French bishop had been deposed since the Liberation, when a few bishops accused of collaborating with the Nazis had been removed. The pope's decision had been made, said Cardinal Gantin as he conveyed the news to Gaillot in January 1995, because the latter had taken no notice over the last ten years of "remarks and warnings made about the way he exercised his episcopal ministry." Some French bishops, such as the bishop of St. Brieuc, were "shocked and pained" by the deposition, and the president of the Protestant Federation of France denounced the "intolerance and sectarian behavior" of the Roman authorities. But Cardinal Jean-Marie Lustiger of Paris said that Gaillot had been "a prisoner of the media" and "deaf to our efforts" to restrain him.

Gaillot himself said, "I hope to work with the poor and outcast. I feel particularly close to them now." It was indeed the manner in which he had taken up the cause of the marginalized that had been one of the chief irritants for those who wanted him removed. He promoted the needs of illegal immigrants and advocated the use of condoms to protect those at risk of AIDS. He signed petitions alongside Communist politicians and made frequent trips to support the Palestinian cause or the black cause in South Africa or to oppose the presence of the Polish Carmelite nuns in Auschwitz. He appeared on saucy television shows and gave interviews to both gay and girlie magazines. He used to say that this was the way he reached the millions of people who never set foot in a church. He was considered beyond reproach on issues of faith and morals, though he did practice, and advocate, intercommunion. Because he refused to resign voluntarily and accept the title of emeritus bishop of Evreux, he was transferred to the titular diocese of Partenia, nominally in Mauritania. He put a brave face on it, explaining that he was now released from the limitations of a geographical boundary and had become bishop of the desert sands and the winds, at the service of anyone who visited his Web site.

The appointment of bishops, and the threats of conformity hanging over them, was a crucial issue, but not the only one. There was also the attempt to take control of theological thinking. Out of a string of encyclicals throughout the pontificate, all of them lengthy and needlessly wordy, the one that made the most headlines for its call to order was *Veritatis Splendor*, leaked in late July 1992, which formulated the basic principles of Catholic moral theology and demanded disciplinary action against moral theologians who dissented. "It is not the best of encyclicals," confessed Belgian Cardinal God-fried Danneels, "but it is an important document." Clearly, the pope would not have written this unless he sincerely believed there was a serious crisis. In any event, it proved that he felt there was still work to be done, work made all the more urgent because his pontificate was entering its final phase.

There was other unfinished business of a disciplinary nature. The question of women's ordination was supposedly put to rest forever in May 1994, when in *Ordinatio Sacerdotalis* John Paul declared that the Church "has no authority whatsoever to confer priestly ordination on women and that this judgment is to be definitively held by all the Church's faithful." The fact that this ploy did not work became obvious when there was a follow-up "Reply to a *Dubium* (Doubt)" in October 1995 from the Congregation for the Doctrine of the Faith, announcing that this is what the ordinary magisterium—the bishops around the world—had always taught and therefore it had been "set forth infallibly."

Certain provinces of the Anglican Communion had been ordaining women since the 1970s, and the Church of England followed suit with its synod decision of November 11, 1992. Some British Anglicans, especially clergy, felt that the Church of England had "no right" to make this decision on its own and were drawn to "cross over" to the Catholic Church. This process was called "swimming the Tiber." Anxious to rebut the charge that they were hopeless misogynists leaving the Church of England merely because of women's ordination, they usually explained that they were not opposed to the ordination of women "as such," but merely declaring a part of the Church did not have the authority to make such a decision on its own. If the "universal Church," presided over by the Bishop of

Rome, were to decide to ordain women, then they would be able to accept it.

The position of the Catholic Church on this question had been stated authoritatively by Pope Paul VI in 1976. He was responding to the Anglican ordinations of that time. He ordered a study of the question from various points of view. The Vatican's own Pontifical Biblical Commission concluded by twelve votes to five that "it does not seem that the New Testament alone will permit us to settle in a clear way and once and for all the problem of the possible accession of women to the priesthood."[4] This no doubt explained the cautious tone of the declaration of the Congregation for the Doctrine of the Faith, *Inter Insigniores,* in 1976. Its key statement was that the Church "does not consider herself authorized to admit women to priestly ordination."

A theologian who is also a cardinal, Carlo Maria Martini, felt able to comment freely as late as April 1993, "The problems, the questions, raised by women's issues, should be taken seriously by both sides. Feminism has a tendency to exaggerate its own message, to see everything from one point of view, and no doubt there are good reasons for this. The Church is part of society, and society develops more rapidly in some sectors than in others." Martini explained that if the Catholic Church were to admit women priests *suddenly,* then there would be a risk of schism, and "the pope has to be concerned with keeping his huge flock with all its different opinions together."

He went on:

As for the issue itself, I think we should come to it little by little, to gradual solutions that will satisfy not only the most progressive but also the majority, while remaining true to tradition and also within the bounds of common sense. That's my opinion. But I can foresee decades of struggle ahead. When

*people ask me, and it's usually Americans: "Will we have
women priests?" I answer: "Not in this millennium."*[5]

Since there were only seven years to go when Martini made
this remark, it could have meant there was not long to wait.
But he might also have meant, "Not for a thousand years."

Perhaps it was this interview and others like it that
spurred John Paul II on to pronounce. At any rate, he
rushed in where Paul VI feared to tread. His encounters
with American nuns, nearly all disastrous, provided another
motive. Right at the start of his pontificate, during his first
visit to the United States in 1979, he had listened in stony
silence as Sister Theresa Kane, then president of the Leadership Conference of Women Religious, urged him "to be
mindful of the intense suffering and pain which is part of
the life of so many women in these United States." She suggested that the Church's message of human dignity and rev-
erence for the human person required that the Church
"respond by providing the possibility of women as persons
being included in *all* the ministries of the Church."

Whatever exactly happened—the acoustics were not very
good in the Washington Shrine of the Immaculate Concep-
tion, and some said the pope did not hear these words—this
early episode set the scenario for the pontificate. As American sisters became more and more aggressive—as Pope
John Paul saw it—so his opposition to them became more
and more extreme. They were accused of importing "secular feminism" and "radical feminism" into the Church.
Besides, they were threatening to bring these themes to the
Synod on Consecrated Life in autumn 1994. That may
explain the timing of the letter.

The apostolic letter *Ordinatio Sacerdotalis* was born of a
sense of mystical, premillennial urgency. This brief five-page
letter was designed to commit the Church definitively.

Counterarguments were not considered. The letter was an act of authority born of irritation that the question "in some places" is considered "still open to debate." Its declaration that the issue is definitively closed was clear, peremptory, brutal, and decisive.

Ordinatio Sacerdotalis summed up the central weakness of the pontificate. It was an act of the monarchical or even "imperial" papacy produced without serious consultation on its contents or its "opportunity." It showed scant regard for ecumenical implications, declaring in effect that in ordaining women the Anglicans had done something that is "impossible." It relied upon obedience rather than persuasion, disciplinary measures rather than explanation. It was scripturally feeble. It treated those who find difficulty in accepting it as dissidents. And when they would not sit down, the "Reply to a *Dubium*" hammered them still harder. But both documents reanimated discussion more than they closed it down.

John Paul tried to cheer up the women the next June by writing them a flowery document saying "thank you" over and over again for "the mystery of woman" and "for all that constitutes the eternal measure of her feminine dignity." He enthused: "Thank you, every woman, for the simple fact of being a woman!" It was well meant, but patronizing and provoked both amusement and bemusement.

Two more encyclicals dropped from the papal pen in 1995. *Evangelium Vitae* presented an apocalyptic view of a world torn between the culture of life and the culture of death, and an encyclical on ecumenical issues, *Ut Unum Sint*, gave some grounds for hope to the other churches when John Paul asked other Christians to "engage with me in a patient and fraternal dialogue" and to work with him in seeking together "the forms in which this [Petrine] ministry may accomplish a service of love." They were warm words, but no evidence of willingness to exercise a different sort of papal role could be observed in practice.

On the contrary, centralism and control became tighter year by year. John Paul II issued an apostolic letter in 1998, *Ad Tuendam Fidem*, that tightened up punishments for doctrinal dissent. But what was even more alarming was the accompanying commentary from Cardinal Ratzinger, which went out of its way to say that the truths of the faith that had been "definitively taught" included not only the impossibility of ordaining women to the priesthood, but also the legitimacy of the election of a pope and the invalidity of Anglican orders. Moreover, those who rejected such doctrines were "no longer in full communion with the Catholic Church."

The same summer saw another repressive document, though bishops around the world have tried to put a positive spin on it. *Apostolos Suos* was an apostolic letter under the pope's name that limited the powers of episcopal conferences, declaring that they were not an expression of collegiality, but derived their authority from their unity with the pope and the universal college of bishops, and that they could not issue statements on moral or doctrinal matters unless these were voted through unanimously or had prior approval from Rome.

Meanwhile there were more attempts to control individual theologians. The stage had been set for this early in the pontificate with the trial-like summons to Rome in December 1979 of the Belgian Dominican theologian Edward Schillebeeckx, who had been an influential *peritus* (theological expert) at Vatican II, and the declaration within the same week that the Swiss theologian Hans Küng "can no longer be considered a Catholic theologian nor function as such," because of his critique of infallibility. Then had come the inquiry into the "father of liberation theology," Peruvian theologian Gustavo Gutiérrez, closely followed by the silencing of the Brazilian liberation theologian Leonardo Boff in April 1985; two Franciscan cardinals from Brazil, Arns and Lorscheider, came with Boff to support him during his face-to-face investigation. In 1984 there had been the Instruction on Certain Aspects of the Theology of Liberation, which condemned the allegedly dangerous this-worldly tendencies of liberation theology, sowing suspicion without mentioning names.

Throughout the pontificate the sea of continuing investigations continued, mostly conducted in secret. U.S. moral theologian Charles Curran lost his license to teach as a Catholic theologian. Then in January 1997 came the infamous excommunication of the Sri Lankan liberation theologian Tissa Balasuriya for his views on original sin following the publication of his book *Mary and Human Liberation*. A personal appeal to the pope fell on deaf ears—John Paul had personally approved the notification of excommunication, it was announced. The Balasuriya case became something of an embarrassment until shortly before the Synod for Asia of April 1998, when the excommunication was lifted. The Vatican presented the solution as a backing down by Balasuriya, but Balasuriya insisted that his expressions of regret were only for the way others had—mistakenly—perceived errors in his writings.

The solution of this case, however, in no way heralded an end to investigations. In October 1998 inquiries began into the work of the learned Jesuit Jacques Dupuis at Rome's Gregorian University, author of a major book, *Toward a Christian Theology of Religious Pluralism*, and later that year into the work of the best-selling Jesuit spiritual writer from India, the late Anthony de Mello, whose book *Sadhana* had explored Christian ways of using Eastern meditation techniques. All three of these cases were marked by a nervousness over interfaith dialogue and a fear that the uniqueness of Christ and the distinctiveness of the Christian doctrine of God were under threat. Meanwhile, the Australian priest and popular writer Paul Collins responded in a more upbeat way to the opening of investigations into his writings on the misuse of Vatican power. Such inquisitions were a help to sales, he pointed out.

Five years after Bishop Norbert Werbs had voiced aloud his misgivings at the First European Synod, Archbishop John Quinn, the recently retired bishop of San Francisco, made a more public appeal for a radical overhaul of the Vatican. He chose as the setting for his critique not Rome or San Francisco, but a quiet Oxford college, the Jesuit house of Campion Hall. Or rather its garden. There, on a blowy afternoon in late June 1996, he stood at a lectern while the sharp wind blew leaves over the spellbound audience and thunder rumbled in the background, as though the gods were angry. He raised the issues of the organization of synods, the appointment of bishops, the translation of the catechism, the decline of priests, clerical celibacy, the role of episcopal conferences, general absolution, divorce, and readmission to the sacraments. The rain held off—just—as he delivered the sort of bombshell address that he could only give *after* he had retired. He said:

> *I am not an angry man. I am not angry at the pope. I am not angry at the Roman Curia. I am not angry at the Church. I have given my whole life to the service of the Church since I was fourteen years old. But I am a grown man now, and all this does not prevent me from seeing what I judge to be defects and things that need adjusting.*

(In late 1999, Quinn went on to publish his book *Reforming the Papacy*, again made possible by the fact that he was no longer in office.)

A couple of years after Quinn's Oxford lecture, Bishop

Peter James Cullinane of Palmerston North delivered another frank address, this time directly to Pope John Paul. Year by year it was becoming obvious not only that things were not getting better, but that the oppression was gathering pace as the pope got older. Cullinane was speaking on behalf of all the New Zealand bishops, at their *ad limina* meeting in 1998, immediately before the 1998 Synod for Oceania:

> *Sometimes we bishops are unable to explain actions which seem inconsistent with the Church's most fundamental commitments.*
>
> *In your encyclical letter* Ut Unum Sint *you courageously invited other Christian leaders to make suggestions about how the Petrine ministry might be exercised. Yet, within the household of the Catholic Church itself, dicasteries of the Holy See occasionally make norms which impinge on the ministry of bishops with little or no consultation of the episcopate as such. This seems inconsistent.*
>
> *In the spirit of the Second Vatican Council, you yourself have reaffirmed the Church's intention to "preserve a proper freedom in the various forms of spiritual life and discipline in the variety of liturgical rites and even the theological elaboration of revealed truth." But that is hardly the experience of Eastern Rite Christians when their priests are evicted from, or not allowed to be ordained within, dioceses of the Latin Rite. Nor do such mechanisms of "control" and "dominance" encourage those who are crying out for great progress in the complex but urgent matter of inculturation.*
>
> *Within the context of your own remarkable contribution to the Church's social teaching, you have often given assurances that the faith cannot be imposed on anyone. But then, within the household of the faith we threaten with penalties those who have difficulties with teachings that the Church itself does not*

teach definitively. . . . We simply ask whether it is appropriate to burden further by the threat of penalties those Catholics who try in good faith to combine their loyalty to the Church with integrity of intellect and conscience. . . .

You yourself have called on "the ecclesial community to foster greater appreciation of women's rights and to enable them to be more actively involved in roles of responsibility." We agree with you, and consider the matter urgent because only when that happens will people more easily see that equality does not derive from, nor depend upon, ordination. We look to the Holy See to exercise leadership by sharing with women all those roles which do not require ordination.

Any such gap that opens up between the values officially proclaimed since Vatican II and the practice of how the Church is actually run creates the sense of frustration and malaise referred to in this comment by the U.S. canon lawyer Ladislas Orsy:

A good deal of what is usually described as postconciliar restlessness is really nothing else than grace-filled vision postulating action. The energy contained in the word received is seeking corresponding action. Thus, our laity have heard that they were the people of God no less than the clergy, and now— no wonder!—they are asking for a more intense sharing in the sacred mission of the Church. Never again will they be satisfied with being told—as they often are—that their vocation is to sanctify secular realities.[6]

Nothing said in this chapter will come as a surprise revelation to any cardinal who has been moderately alert during the last fifteen years. But the rare courage shown by Bishop Werbs, Archbishop Quinn, and Bishop Cullinane is beyond the reach of the cardinals, who are in such a special way the pope's closest colleagues. For them, even more than for the bishops, "loyalty to the Holy Father" is paramount. They keep resolutely mum. Privately there are some, even among this bunch carefully handpicked for their support of the present regime, who think otherwise. If so, such private thoughts are being saved up for the next conclave. That will be the right time, the *kairos*, for cardinals to speak.

Jesuit Tom Reese, of the Woodstock Center, Georgetown University, spent 1993–94 in Rome studying the Roman Curia. His view is that the next conclave may be the most difficult and perhaps protracted of modern times. The reason is that this time the cardinals know one another better than ever before: they have watched one another perform and know one another's strengths and weaknesses. They no longer need to rely on the Roman Curia to tell them what to think. In any case, never has the Italian proportion been so low. The 120 cardinals (less a few who have died) will go into the conclave knowing that they carry with them the voices of all those outside. Too many voices are excluded from the conclave—the voices of the local churches from four continents, of women, of the young or even the middle-aged, and above all of the poor. These voices are not a distant muffled echo. They are the very heart of the Church. So the college of cardinals, very properly concerned with the credibility of the Church in the modern world, will have to bring in these diverse voices and relay them.

It is time for a new style. A conclave is a moment of freedom, a chance for the Church to make a fresh start.

SIX The Perils of a Non-Italian

There is one more thing that can be said for sure about the next pope: he will be—give or take some obscure or doubtful candidates—the 265th successor of St. Peter.

Do the origins of the popes conform to any cultural or geographical pattern? The following table summarizes their background:

Origin	As a percent of 264
Rome	37.5
Italy (minus Rome)	40.9
Greece/Asia Minor	6.8
Africa	1.1
Europe (minus Italy)	12.5 (6.4 French)
Other (and unknown)	1.2[1]

A few comments on this table. If we add together the Romans and the Italians (using the term for the peninsula), we reach 78.4 percent, a not unreasonable figure for the Bishop of Rome.

The "Greek" period of dominance is crammed into the years between 654 and 752, when eight out of seventeen popes came from the Middle East, mostly Syrian monks driven westward by the onslaught of Islam. The 6.4 percent French popes also fall within a narrow time band, between 999 and 1378, when there were seventeen of them. Seven of the French popes came between 1305 and 1378, the result of the "Gallican" policies of Philippe le Bel, who installed the papacy firmly at Avignon in France.

There were only three "Germans," three Spaniards, and one Englishman, Nicholas Breakspear, who became Hadrian IV (1154–59). Born in Abbots Langley, near St. Albans, son of a humble clerk who later became a monk of St. Albans, Breakspear made his name as a diplomat in Scandinavia. A friend of the political philosopher John of Salisbury, who thought Thomas Becket could have been more accommodating and witnessed his murder in Canterbury Cathedral, Breakspear was said to be able to accept criticism. It was in his pontificate, however, that the possibly blasphemous title "Vicar of Christ" first became common. The Irish remember him as the man who blessed Henry II's attempt to incorporate Ireland in his kingdom. So much for the last and only English pope.

The last non-Italian was Hadrian VI, 1522–23. Between him and John Paul II was a gap of 455 years. Not for nothing is the phrase, "We think in centuries here," a favorite in the Vatican. After John Paul II, should the experiment be repeated so soon? Choosing a non-Italian pope may appear a forward-looking and broad-minded choice. It seemed so when John Paul II was elected in 1978, and it seemed so when the last non-Italian Pope, Hadrian VI, was elected in 1522. But though Hadrian was a man of great talent and goodness, as a pope he was a disaster. What is more, he was a disaster precisely because he was a non-Italian.

Hadrian Florensz (or Florenszoon) of Utrecht was educated by the Brethren of the Common Life—a community that stressed the sincere, interior piety of the Devotio Moderna movement, which is known mostly through Thomas à Kempis's devotional classic *The Imitation of Christ*. Hadrian was a distinguished scholar. He had been some thirty years at Louvain University, and Erasmus described him as a *scholastique des pieds à la tête*, "a scholar from head to toe."

He became tutor to the future King Charles V of Spain, then in 1516 bishop of Tortosa, and cardinal the following year, on Charles's recommendation. He was appointed inquisitor general for much of northern Spain, and by 1520 Charles was leaving him as viceroy of Spain in order to take up the position of Holy Roman Emperor.

It was in Spain in 1522 that Hadrian heard of his election as pope. He had been chosen to break a deadlock and was the first non-Italian pope since 1378. The Roman crowds were furious at the choice of a foreigner and feared he would live in Spain or Germany and not come to Rome at all. They hung a placard on the Vatican reading "This palace to let." But elsewhere in Europe the news was welcomed, and it was said that he was not only a man of great learning, but the most pious of all the cardinals.

Because of the travel difficulties of the age, it took seven months for Hadrian to arrive in Rome, but when he did so, on August 29, 1522, the crowds turned out with joy and enthusiasm. Not only were they relieved to find him come at all, but they were struck by the charisma of his grave piety. He had the Blessed Sacrament carried in procession into Rome before him, so that homage would be paid to God rather than to him.

According to early impressions, "he was given to silence, cautious and to the point in his speech; humble, learned, chaste, upright, alert in conversation, kind, quiet and understanding to those who see him and talk with him, truthful in what he says, just in his judgments." It was said that "even his smile has a tinge of seriousness." Another early observer enthused: "If you were to see the angelic face of the pontiff, and hear his sweet voice and observe his cere-monies, you would think him rather something divine than a human being."[2]

On his third day in Rome Hadrian held his first consis-tory. He impressed the cardinals with his simple attire—a cope and miter—and delivered a speech "with great dignity and at great length" and "with such majesty, such sincerity, and moreover such alertness that his speech seemed to everyone as faith-filled as it was beautiful." He said he had "never asked for, never hoped for, never imagined this dig-nity, and God knew that after acceptance had never taken pleasure in it." Indeed, had he not been convinced that it could be for the good of the Church, he would have rejected the offer.

The office of pope, he said, was one of "shepherd, to lead back the sheep who were wandering, to strengthen those who were weak and to confirm those who were healthy." But if he were to make mistakes or use his office for unworthy ends, he wished to "be corrected and put right" and "would listen patiently to the admonitions of his brothers."

After such a promising start, what went wrong? The problem was in the clash of values between Hadrian's aus-tere spirituality and the more flamboyant expectations of the Romans. In his speech at the first consistory, he said that "justice and morality were sought from the city of Rome," but "good morals had so dissolved that in their place vices were rampant, the practice of which was so familiar to all that now they are not even considered vices anymore."

His attempts at moral reform stirred up enormous resentment. He issued an edict banning all disorderly people from Rome and proscribing the wearing of arms. A second edict forbade ecclesiastics to wear beards on the grounds that it made them look like soldiers. (This could be seen as a contemporary parallel to John Paul's attempt to stop clergy and religious wearing secular dress.) And Hadrian tightened up on the freedom with which pardons for murder were granted: in the future such pardons would "not be given except for very weighty reasons, and after hearing the case of the injured parties." The reaction to such discipline in Rome was one of fear. "Everyone trembles," reported the Venetian ambassador, "and all the cardinals have put off their beards."

He was concerned, also, to root out corruption from the judges of the Roman Rota, for, he said, "it was a scandal to the whole world that justice was administered by them under the influence of large sums of money." Another plea he made was for "peace between Christian princes," and he urged a common Christian front "against the infidel," for the Turks were besieging Rhodes at the time.

Later the same month Hadrian wrote a briefing to the nuncio at the imperial Diet of Nuremberg, in which he urged the Christian princes to unite in another battle—against Lutheranism. He condemned Lutherans for their "enormous scandals, disturbances, plundering of goods, homicides, quarrels and dissensions," for their "blasphemies, curses, gibes and bitterness," and for what he saw as their loose marriage ethics.

It may be surprising that such a learned theologian focused attention on condemning Lutheran morals rather than discussing their theology. But Hadrian's attitude was that theological disputes were settled by reference to the magisterium, not by private argument. True teaching is found in what has been affirmed by "the General Councils and the universal Church," he said, "whom God never permits to err in matters of faith."

So far Hadrian displays a stunning similarity to John Paul II—in intellect, talent, impressive public charisma, lengthy speeches, proclamations of high moral standards, unquestioning faith in the magisterium, and a sense of vocation to bring back the erring members of the flock. But there were differences too—in Hadrian's attempt to rein in Vatican expenditure, in his lack of fluency in languages, and in his philistine approach to the arts.

Hadrian attended to economic reform partly to deal with the high level of Vatican debt run up by his predecessors and partly because of his own background in Devotio Moderna with its simpler lifestyle. He cut the number of papal grooms from one hundred to four, though he was then prevailed upon to raise it back to twelve so as not to have fewer than an ordinary cardinal. He made cuts in the Vatican expenditure on corn, with the result that one employee, his livelihood threatened, tried to stab him.

Hadrian's problems in having his ideas accepted were compounded by the fact that he spoke poor Italian, and the Romans saw his austerity as a lack of culture. He visited the shrines of the martyrs in Rome, but spurned the pagan remains. Popes had traditionally been patrons of the arts, but Hadrian's comment on the Laocoön composition was that such works were "after all, only the effigies of heathen idols." He stopped the paintings being executed in the Hall of Constantine, and Raphael's pupils had to look for work elsewhere. He also let it be known that he wished the triumphal arch being built in his honor to be discontinued.

He made no secret of his dislike of poetry, considering

that anyone who appreciated religious writing would have no time for such frivolities. After his death the poets got their revenge, circulating the following lines:

Hadrian, treacherous as the sea,
Hypocrite, cruel, envious, miserly,
Hateful to all, dear to none,
Enchanter, magician, idolater, hollow,
Rustic, disgraceful, inhuman,
Liar, deceiver, thief, poultry-keeper,
Solitary, bestial and a sorcerer.

Hadrian's economic cuts had led to the charge of being "miserly" and "cruel." He was "treacherous" for going back on the normal Vatican financial commitments, and "rustic" or a "poultry-keeper" for his lack of appreciation for Renaissance arts. His "solitary" lifestyle—in fact a disciplined dedication to work and prayer—was not appreciated as a virtue; the charges of being an "enchanter" may refer to the spell of his personality.

Pressures other than moral reform built up for Hadrian. Rome was suffering from the plague, and it increased to the point where a hundred were dying each day. Hadrian's sense of duty, however, prevented him moving to safety outside the city.

Then Rhodes fell to the Turks. On January 28, 1523, a messenger from Archduke Ferdinand of Austria chided the pope for neglecting to help Rhodes under siege "when a little money would have been enough to save that place." He warned that, as a result, it would be "difficult or impossible to defend Hungary, Croatia and the remaining Christian republics." "For the defense of the Christian faith you have not the money," he complained. "You ought to sell everything you have, including sacred objects. The patrimony of the Church is the patrimony of the martyrs."

As he listened to this attack, Hadrian's face became so agitated that many of those present had difficulty restraining their laughter. He fell into deep gloom, and Hadrian protested that the cardinals "had called him to torments, to prison." He worked hard that year to set up of a league of defense against the Turks, comprising the emperor and many other rulers, "for the defense of the Christian religion."

A treaty along these lines was formally read out at Santa Maria Maggiore on August 5, 1523. But Hadrian returned from the ceremony to the Vatican in a great sweat, with a complete loss of appetite. His illness lasted forty days, and he died on September 14, which was a most fitting date for the death of such a pious and tormented man—the feast of the Exaltation of the Cross.

Many said he had been poisoned, for his illness was not satisfactorily diagnosed, and the swelling of the corpse observed by those who came to pay homage reminded them of the appearance of others who had been poisoned. But an autopsy provided no clear evidence of poison, and the doctor attributed the death to melancholy. It is now thought likely that the cause of death was a kidney infection and blood poisoning, with—or more probably without—the assistance of poison.

The sudden rise and scarcely less rapid fall of Hadrian VI are a salutary reminder of the difficulties that may be faced when a foreigner, however worthy, steps into a Church culture very different from his own. People have sympathized with one side or the other, seeing Hadrian as a humorless killjoy or the Romans as stubborn and corrupt. But at the heart of this brief incident, lasting barely more than a year, is a human tragedy in which it is not easy to apportion blame. Plague, schism, war, and simple misunderstanding conspired together to destroy and discredit a truly talented, impressive, and holy man.

It is little wonder that the experiment of a non-Italian pope was not tried again for more than four a half centuries. John Paul II has passed with flying colors in some areas where Hadrian failed—in linguistic facility and in simply enjoying the job. But the drawbacks of culture clash have plagued his pontificate in much the same way as they did Hadrian's. Both men were brilliant in intellect and spirituality and charisma, but both men failed to understand and appreciate a society that was foreign to them. Their eyes were blind to the virtues of the culture they were determined to reform.

After the experiment of a pope from Poland, the cardinals will have to decide whether they dare risk another non-Italian straightaway. No matter how holy or how talented the candidate, a non-Italian can be a misfit, and even a total disaster.

PART II THE CANDIDATES

SEVEN Electors as Runners

This chapter, finally, will look at the electors, who are, by definition, the candidates. Cardinals are made in batches, through an event called a consistory. Pope John Paul II has held seven consistories at intervals of approximately every three years:

Date	Number of Cardinals
June 30, 1979	14
February 2, 1983	18
May 25, 1985	28
June 28, 1988	24
June 28, 1991	22
November 26, 1994	30
February 21, 1998	20 (plus 2 *in pectore*)

Adding up the right-hand list, one finds that John Paul has "created" a grand total of 158 cardinals. This is a "record." However, quite a number are now dead. Others are over eighty and therefore cannot vote (some were even over eighty when they were appointed). The maximum number of electors permitted is 120. As we go to press there are 156 cardinals, if we count those *in pectore* whose names are not published. This number is always going down slowly because of the trickle of deaths, while it only goes up in lurches when there is a consistory to make a new batch of cardinals.

Of these 156 cardinals, 106 will be under eighty on January 1, 2000, and eligible to take part in the next conclave. Out of these, John Paul II has appointed 94, with the remaining 12 appointed by Paul VI (Aponte, Arns, Baum, Gantin, Kim, Lorscheider, Otunga, Ratzinger, Sales, Sin, Taofinu'u, and Thiandoum).

And so, whatever happens inside the conclave, no one is going to have had more influence upon its outcome than the one man who will not be there: John Paul II. He cannot choose his successor, but he has chosen the people who will choose his successor.

How well do cardinals know each other? A novelty of this pontificate is that it has given the cardinals a chance to get to know each other better than ever before. Hitherto they had met only in "consistories" and during conclaves. Pope John Paul II brought them together for special meetings as part of his desire "to join them more closely to the pastoral mission of Peter."

There have been five such consultations on the following themes:

November 4–9, 1979. Wealthy churches to come to the aid of poor ones.

November 23–26, 1982. The "reform" of the Roman Curia and finance. It was a crisis meeting on the latter topic. The press had raised the question of how far the IOR (Institute of Religious Works, commonly, the Vatican Bank) was involved in the crash of the Banco Ambrosiano.

November 20–22, 1985. Immediately preceding the Synod on Vatican II. John Paul II defended the Curia against its critics. Cardinal Ratzinger spoke on primacy and collegiality, and Cardinal Jerôme Hamer on episcopal conferences, which were to be cut down to size.

April 4–6, 1991. Inroads made by the "sects" especially in Latin America. Cardinal Ratzinger announced one authoritative document, possibly an encyclical, on moral questions and another on the defense of life.

June 13–14, 1994. How to celebrate the year 2000. An ecumenical meeting of Jews, Christians, and Muslims on Mount Sinai. Repentance for mistakes of the past millennium. Also to prepare for the Cairo conference.

These meetings were unprecedented. To take the college of cardinals thus seriously was, at first blush, an original feature of this pontificate. But it could be considered a rival institution to the Synod of Bishops established by Pope Paul VI, which is a collegial body in the spirit (and letter) of Vatican II. Present at synods are presidents of episcopal conferences. Many of them are cardinals, but this is not a qualification for the job.

There have been six synods of this pontificate that have taken themes as their topics:

1980, The Role of the Christian Family. Intended by Pope John Paul II as a defense of *Humanae Vitae*, it instead subtly undermined it by calling for a "deeper understanding" of it and an examination of the concept of *intrinsece inhonestum* ("intrinsically dishonorable"), which *Humanae Vitae* consciously and deliberately preferred to *Casti Connubii*'s *intrinsece malum* ("intrinsically evil").

1983, Reconciliation and Penance. The aim here was to call into question concepts such as "social sin," which seems to undermine personal sin, and also to manifest opposition to "general absolution," although this was a permissible form of the sacrament of Reconciliation foreseen by the reforms of Vatican II.

1985, called the Extraordinary Synod, because it was not in the regular series. Its purpose was both to "celebrate" and to qualify Vatican II. Fundamentally it confirmed Vatican II, but was pessimistic about "the signs of the times" and the collegial reality of episcopal conferences.

1987, The Role of the Laity in the Church and the World. An exciting synod, involving much participationof the laity in advance in the developed world—none elsewhere.

1990, The Role of the Priest. The principal aim of this synod was to defend clerical celibacy and to oppose requests for the ordination of married men.

1994, The Consecrated Life. A curious title, devised so that "secular institutes" could be included along with religious, monks, friars, and nuns. Basil Hume presided. The idea of temporary vows was floated. U.S. sisters who refused the sacraments from "male priests" were trounced.

But in addition to the thematic synods, a characteristic of the last years of the millennium has been a succession of continental synods, which have brought together bishops from particular regions of the world. These have been as follows:

1980, Netherlands
1991, First European Synod
1994, Africa
1995, Lebanon
1997, America
1998, Asia
1998, Oceania
1999, Second European Synod

True, the *motive* behind these meetings was not to enable the cardinals to get to know each other better. It was to organize their support for the projects of the pontificate. Some synods involved "delicate" matters such as finance—not to be discussed among consenting adults in public. But from the point of view of this book, the main effect of such meetings was to make the cardinals better informed about the life of the Church. For Cardinal Carlo Maria Martini, archbishop of Milan, this novelty in the history of the Church has greatly strengthened unity:

> There never was such a tangible, strong and—one may say—affective unity. I see this quite clearly in the fraternity and communion among the bishops which flowered at Vatican II and later in the synods. This is a very important "sign of the times" that was not there—or hardly there—in the past. The bishops knew each other then, but not well. Now they visit each other, meet and come together in unity.[1]

Martini was speaking of bishops, but the same applies to cardinals. As he said, they have a chance to meet each other at synods every three years. Observers got into the habit in the pontificate of Paul VI of describing synods as "dress rehearsals for the next conclave." There is still some truth in this, especially toward the end of a pontificate.

No one, of course, officially "runs for pope." But there are unofficial ways—lectures, press interviews, and travel—by which a cardinal can discreetly propose his candidacy while denying that anything untoward is happening. Yet obviously cardinals cannot be condemned to Trappist silence, and it would be a grotesque distortion to judge everything they do in the light of a forthcoming conclave that may not happen anytime soon.

With these provisos in mind, we will look at the contenders. A few years ago, there seemed a few strong and obvious candidates, but as those men become older, the field looks very open indeed. Despite the unusually large number of candidates on paper, it is hard to find anyone who is quite right for the job, so all must be considered. It will turn out rather easier to say who will not be elected than who will be.

For all practical purposes the candidates are the cardinals. In theory they could elect someone who was not a cardinal, even someone who was not a bishop, or even a priest, so long as he was male and therefore thought capable of being ordained to the priesthood and episcopacy (this is what happened in Frederick Rolfe's novel *Hadrian VII*). But in practice a candidate would need to be inside the conclave where the electors can have a good look at each other and be swayed this way and that: the election of someone outside the conclave is impractical.

This means that out of the 156 cardinals, we can straightaway strike off all the cardinals who will be over eighty at the turn of the millennium. (From now on, all ages will be given in relation to this date of January 1, 2000.) Quite apart from being too old to do the job, they will not be inside the conclave. This brings our list down by nearly one-third. The best known of these old men include Paolo Dezza (ninety-eight), who is almost as old as the century and who was controversially imposed on the Jesuits in 1981 when John Paul II wanted to alter the line taken by the saintly Jesuit General Pedro Arrupe. Another well-known over-eighty-year-old is the Irish Cahal Brendan Daly (eighty-two), foe of the IRA during some of the worst years of the troubles in Northern Ireland. Then there is the distinguished ecumenist Johannes Willebrands (ninety), former president of the Pontifical Council for Promoting Christian Unity. Also the equally distinguished opinion-former Franz König (ninety-four), formerly archbishop of Vienna and also a former president of the Pontifical Council for Dialogue with Non-believers; he had been a kingmaker at the time of John Paul's election, and his voice is still listened to with great respect today—to the extent that when, in the London *Tablet*, he challenged the inquisitorial actions against the Jesuit Jacques Dupuis taken by the Congregation for the Doctrine of the Faith, Cardinal Ratzinger was moved to make a public reply (January 16 and March 13, 1999). But the most infamous cardinal to slip mercifully over the age border is the Austrian Hans Hermann Groër (eighty), also a former archbishop of Vienna. His homosexual liaisons and abuses of young monks (he is a Benedictine) provoked one of the biggest scandals the European Church has ever seen, spurring the formation of the international reform movement We Are Church.

Many of the over-eighties are Italians, made cardinals before it became imperative to internationalize the Curia. There is the oddball Silvio Oddi (eighty-nine), sometime prefect of the Congregation for the Clergy, who broke convention by speaking out in 1996 about how Cardinal Ratzinger would certainly be his candidate if he were allowed to vote: "I like his way of doing things, his intelligence, his faith." Too bad, Oddi has no vote. We also eliminate Fiorenzo Angelini (eighty-three), Corrado Bafile (ninety-six), Paolo Bertoli (ninety-one), Giovanni Canestri (eighty-one), Giuseppe Caprio (eighty-five), Giuseppe Casoria (ninety-one), Giovanni Cheli (eighty-one), Vincenzo Fagiolo (eighty-one), Angelo Felici (eighty), Antonio Innocenti (eighty-four), Pietro Palazzini (eighty-seven), Salvatore Pappalardo (eighty-one), Luigi Poggi (eighty-two), Egano Righi-Lambertini (ninety-three), Opilio Rossi (eighty-nine), Aurelio Sabattani (eighty-seven), Giuseppe Maria Sensi (ninety-two), Ersilio Tonini (eighty-five), and Corrado Ursi (ninety-one).

Additional names to eliminate are Gerald Emmett Carter (eighty-seven) and Louis-Albert Vachon (eighty-seven), who are Canadian, the retired archbishops of Toronto and Quebec, respectively. Edouard Gagnon (eighty-one) is also Canadian—a former president of the Pontifical Council for the Family. Juan Carlos Aramburu (eighty-seven) and Francisco Primatesta Raúl (eighty) are Argentinian. Ernesto Corripio Ahumada (eighty) is Mexican. José Alí Lebrún Moratinos (eighty) is from Venezuela. Bernardino Echeverría Ruiz (eighty-seven) is from Ecuador. Juan Francisco Fresno Larrain (eighty-five) is from Chile. Ignatius Kung Pin-mei (ninety-eight) is Chinese. Paul Joseph Pham Dinh Tung (eighty) is Vietnamese. Jean Margéot (eighty-three) is from Mauritius. Paul Zoungrana (eighty-two) is from Burkina Faso. Alfons Maria Stickler (eighty-nine) is Austrian. Marcelo González Martín (eighty-one) and Angel Suquía Goicoechea (eighty-three) are Spanish. Paul Gouyon (eighty-nine) is French. Paul Augustin Mayer (eighty-eight) is German. Adam Kozlowiecki (eighty-eight) is Polish. Franjo Kuharic (eighty) is Croatian. Myroslav Ivan Lubachivsky (eighty-five) is from Ukraine. Kasimierz Swiatek (eighty-five) is from Estonia. Alexandru Todea (eighty-seven) is Romanian.

We can also strike off the cardinals *in pectore* (Latin) or *in petto* (Italian), that is, whose names are held in secret by the pope, because of delicate political circumstances. The current *in pectore* cardinals might be Archbishop Tadeusz Kondrusiewicz, apostolic administrator for European Russia, whose appointment might upset the Orthodox; or perhaps Archbishop Henri Tessier of Algeria, whose life could be in great danger if he were made a cardinal; or maybe the Latin patriarch of Jerusalem, Michel Sabbah, whose nomination might have upset Israel. But whoever these *in pectore* cardinals are, they could not turn up at a conclave without revealing their identity, and since no one knows who they are, they can hardly be candidates for the papacy.

The list is now mercifully thinned out to 106, 12 fewer than the maximum number of cardinal electors permitted, which is 120. We will now divide up the remaining cardinals according to geography: Italians, other Europeans, Latin Americans, Africans, and Asians.

The Italians

We begin with Italians because that is, after all, the custom of centuries. Italians have felt for centuries that the bishop of Rome should be one of them, and they are still a powerful force, even though no longer a technical majority in the conclave. They still have a proprietorial sense that they should give permission before the central diocese of their country passes into the hands of foreigners. And after all, the pope lives in Italy and the Curia operates in Italian. An Italian must be the first, obvious choice, at the very least.

The Italians are a conservative bunch, but that need not deter the cardinal electors, who are themselves a conservative bunch. The exception is of course Cardinal Carlo Maria **Martini,** archbishop of Milan, whom we have already met and who is probably the best-known cardinal in the world after Cardinal Ratzinger, principally because of the number of people, disappointed with John Paul's papacy, who clutch at the name of Martini as the man who will make it all come right again. Aged seventy-two at the dawn of the millennium, he is no wild progressive, as the press might sometimes seem to imply as they search for the slightest chink of disagreement with the official line in which to insert their wedge. The cardinals know Martini is no dangerous liberal, even if he is to the left of most of them. They are also aware that he is the most talented and experienced of the Italians. His election as president of the CCEE (*Consilium Conferentiarum Episcopalium Europae,* or Council of European Episcopal Conferences) is some indication of the international respect he commands, not only as a pastor and administrator, but also as an intellectual. Because of his fame, there is no risk that people will overlook him as a candidate. But he is not flashy—on the contrary, rather a dry Martini—though with great stature.

Martini is a biblical scholar who was rector of the Jesuit university in Rome, the Gregorian, until he was sent to be bishop of Milan in 1979. So he is unusual in being a progressive appointment by John Paul II; most of the progressive bishops were appointed by Paul VI. In Milan he has tried rather unsuccessfully to keep a lowish profile; at least he has tried to keep Milan from being seen as an alternative power base to Rome. But he can never quite hide his intelligence and his leadership qualities. All the same, he has declared that he would only leave Milan to retire to Jerusalem, but that kind of prudent disclaimer of further ambition is routine and need not be taken seriously. When someone has been labeled in advance as a papal contender, it is barely possible to say anything without it being interpreted as an election manifesto. That was already happening at a conference in Jerusalem in February 1994, when he was intended to talk about "religious leadership." After all, the papal office is the supreme instance of "religious leadership." If one didn't know the man, Martini's speech on "religious leadership" could have been seen as a papal election manifesto.

Not for a moment should we think that it was. Yet Martini stated some basic principles the next conclave will have to bear in mind. The first is the distinctive nature of religious leadership according to Luke's Gospel: "The kings of the Gentiles exercise lordship over them; and those in authority are called benefactors. But not so with you; rather let the greatest among you become as the youngest, and the leader as one who serves" (Luke 22:25–26). Next, Martini distinguished three levels of problems that any religious leader has to face: internal problems, concerned with, say, lack of vocations or ministers; left-right tensions within the religious community; and "the problem of development." What on earth was he talking about? Various interviews suggest that he was thinking, for example, about birth control, the ordination of married men, or the ordination of women. Martini is not accurately described as a liberal. But he does not regard all questions as settled in advance.

But preoccupation with these internal problems—Martini went on—should not lead the Church leader to overlook or ignore the problems thrown up by modern society, such as war, violence, defense of human life, abortion, illness, hunger and starvation, the great immigrations, the problem of ecology, tensions in society connected with the beginning and the end of life, bio-ethical problems, and so on. Well, one might say, anyone can make a list. True. But it helps to have the right list, marking priorities. There remain transcendent problems, continued Martini, which are the main specific themes of our religions: "God, salvation, prayer, adoration, faith and hope, forgiveness, life after death, justice and charity, and so on." "I do not want to impose my solution to this question," said Martini, but "we are convinced that these questions are the real vital issues for humanity, and that every other question, no matter how important it appears, depends ultimately on these questions and themes." Martini takes us beyond the conservative-liberal divide—for him a minor internal matter that can be resolved—toward an understanding of what the Church is for.

Martini must still muster a lot of votes. But whether he can gain enough to win looks very doubtful. Against him is that he is a Jesuit. There has never been a Jesuit pope in history; more than that, there has never been a serious Jesuit contender for the papacy either. This need not be decisive, though many are cautious of giving more power to the Jesuits; they are the largest male religious order, and their General has been jokingly called "the black pope" to indicate the fear of a rival power structure.

We could almost speak of a Stop Martini campaign as the number of conservative candidates has risen, and as the rules of the CCEE were changed in such a way that he lost its presidency by being excluded as a member. Against him are not only his views, but also his reputation. The cardinals may know full well that he is no dangerous liberal. But so long as the media trumpet him as the overthrow candidate of the old regime, a vote for him might send a message to the world that the present cardinals do not want to give.

If all this were not enough to block Martini decisively, his mounting age would be likely do the trick. He will be nearly seventy-three on January 1, 2000. Year by year Martini looks less and less likely. He has been the great but fragile hope of progressive—and even moderate—elements in the church for around fifteen years. That hope has to continue to diminish the closer he gets to seventy-five.

The cardinal secretary of state, Angelo **Sodano** (also seventy-two), is beyond doubt the most limited secretary of state of the twentieth century. Compared with his predecessor, Cardinal Agostino Casaroli, whose swan song was his signing of the Treaty of Paris in December 1990, he is a novice who has not yet won respect from the diplomats accredited to the Holy See. His only foreign experience was as nuncio in Chile during the reign of General Augusto Pinochet, whose friend he remains. Sodano is an embarrassment: "a gray man with gray ideas," said one observer.

An astonishing move took Sodano to Santo Domingo in September 1992 to preside over the Conference of Latin American Bishops. He should not have been present at all. The secretary of state should be above intrachurch conflicts.

Since the French Cardinal Jean Villot (1969–79), the first postconciliar secretary of state, his role has been to promote communion between the local Churches. By presiding at Santo Domingo, Sodano forfeited any claims to evenhandedness, rashly committed himself on the conservative side, acted as the hatchet man for the pope, and so lost all credibility. He also has a foul temper. At one point he was so angry with the Latin American bishops that he locked himself in his hotel room and declared his intention of going back to Rome immediately. He was only persuaded to stay by notes pushed under his door. Not to be underestimated as an operator, he is more of a kingmaker than *papabile*.

If you ask someone in the Curia who he thinks will be the next pope, he is quite likely to say Giacomo **Biffi** (seventy-one), archbishop of Bologna. Intelligent but very conservative, he is known as the most intransigent of the Italian cardinals and could be the choice of the powerful conservative groupings like Opus Dei and Comunione e Liberazione. As a diocesan bishop who has never worked in the Vatican (though he is a member of four dicasteries), he could be presented as a "pastoral" bishop rather than just a depressing bureaucrat. But bureaucrat or not, he is still depressing. He is an advocate of firm Catholic positions and opponent of liberal causes like feminism, pacifism, and gay rights. A Church of dialogue, in his view, is "a Church with AIDS, because it no longer has antibodies, and has lost the capacity to resist attack." Doubt is "a malady of the spirit." And on the subject of human rights, his compassion is aroused by the French aristocracy who went to the guillotine.

Another intelligent conservative, but this time of a more suitable age, is the moral theologian Dionigi **Tettamanzi** (sixty-five), archbishop of Genoa. A former secretary-general of the Italian bishops' conference, he looks a plausible candidate on paper, largely because his age is right and he is a prudent man. But he is dull, and will never be able to escape his description (by Archbishop Keith O'Brien of Edinburgh to the press at the Second Synod for Europe) as "a wee, fat guy." His name, "bull's tits," is also a drawback. He may be seen as too close to the old regime: he helped draft the two encyclicals *Veritatis Splendor* and *Evangelium Vitae* and has worked closely not only with John Paul II, but also with Cardinal Camillo **Ruini** (sixty-eight), who in his turn is John Paul's right-hand man as vicar-general for the diocese of Rome. Ruini's rise under John Paul has been meteoric. He has been president of the Italian bishops' conference since 1991, the year in which he was given the responsibility of *relator*, or chief speaker and summarizer, at the First Synod for Europe, with the agenda of bringing the Eastern European Church out of the catacombs to counterbalance the watered-down secularism of Western Europe. Ruini is much disliked, which is often the fate of a court favorite. A wiry, energetic man, he is seen as ruthless, cold, and controlling, with a centralizing agenda. He is likely to be a kingmaker, rather than a candidate.

A more intriguing possibility, though near the upper age limit, would be Marco **Cé** (seventy-four), patriarch of Venice, a moderate conservative who has learned to keep his head down and his mouth shut. Once inside the conclave, his tongue may be loosed and he could play a significant role in mapping out a future direction or even, conceivably, become a candidate himself. He has praised John XXIII (one of his predecessors as patriarch of Venice, as was also John Paul I) as a man "from whom we should learn to have the courage of vision. Like St. Peter, he knew how to preach at Pentecost. Everyone understood him in their own language, because it was the language of love, the universal language." His view of the Church is of a multiplicity of ministries, and his view of the world is of "the dwelling-place of the Son of God."

It is reasonable to assume that those over seventy-five are unlikely to get the job, though a salutary warning is given us in the case of John XXIII, who was elected at the age of seventy-six. Subsequently, the one-month pontificate of John Paul I in 1978 alerted the cardinals to the inconvenience of electing someone who is at risk of dropping down dead. And he was only sixty-five. After that, they dared not elect anyone who seemed at the end of his life. But some of the over-seventy-fives merit a little attention before we strike them off our list.

One of the most famous cardinals over seventy-five is Pio **Laghi** (seventy-seven), a smooth and gentlemanly Italian, made cardinal in 1991 as the reward for a diplomatic career that included the key positions of nuncio to Argentina and the United States. He is now prefect of the Congregation for Catholic Education, though some say he is intellectually lightweight. He cannot go on forever. Most devastating to his chances, however, even more than his age, is the damage to his reputation by the Mothers of the Plaza de Mayo, the group of mothers of the disappeared in Argentina who used to parade in the Buenos Aires square. They said that he was a collaborator with the dirty war of the 1970s, in which around twenty thousand people disappeared. The evidence for this has never been clear. It is not denied that he was a tennis partner of one of the three generals of the military junta, Admiral Massera, and that he married his son and baptized his grandson. But though this would slant him toward taking an uncritical view of his friend's role, playing tennis as such is not a crime. Pio Laghi himself has issued a detailed rebuttal of the charges—"Perhaps I was not a hero, but I was certainly not an accomplice," he said—and his reputation on that score has been stoutly defended by the director of the Catholic aid agency for England and Wales, Julian Filochowski. But whatever the truth of the matter, some mud will always stick. No matter how extensive Laghi's international experience, no matter how good his languages, no matter how convincing his self-justification, no matter how agreeably conservative (to the other cardinals) his opinions, it is stretching credibility to think that they would elect a seventy-seven-year-old whose reputation has once been dragged through the filth of the dirty war.

Achille **Silvestrini** (seventy-six) is another Italian curial cardinal we should now regard as too old—a pity since he is one of the decent, open-minded appointments left over from the time of Paul VI. At first John Paul II seemed not to know what to do with Silvestrini, a man trained in Vatican diplomacy in the school of Cardinal Agostino Casaroli. Eventually, in 1988, he was made a cardinal, and in May 1991 he was appointed prefect of the Congregation for the Oriental Churches, a poisoned chalice he took up at the most difficult moment—after the Gulf War and with Christians emigrating from Lebanon and elsewhere in droves. But Silvestrini has the air of a man who is sidelined and impotent within the Curia.

One of Silvestrini's attractive features is that he was a genuine "friend of the family" of Federico Fellini, the great fantasist and filmmaker. He presided at his funeral Mass in 1993 and defined Fellini as "the lord of images" whose poetic power could transform people and everyday realities. (The images included a savage caricature of the Roman Curia, ridiculed in a fashion parade of disembodied vestments.) "It is poetry," Silvestrini said, and if Fellini had criticized the Church, he had always done so "with irony and with love," accompanied by "an affectionate regard for the defenseless and the humble." It was an absolution, if not a beatification, and made a great contrast with the lofty moralizing of the encyclical *Veritatis Splendor*, issued three months earlier. Actress Giulietta Masina, Fellini's wife of fifty years and a devout Catholic, dressed in white "because Federico could not stand mourning." She leaned for support on her brother Mario and clutched her rosary throughout the Requiem Mass. At the end Silvestrini came down and kissed her hands reverently. Not only is Silvestrini too old to be a plausible choice, but he would also get little support from his curial colleagues. He has hinted he will vote for Martini.

Less well known than either Pio Laghi or Silvestrini outside Italy, but still worth consideration, is Silvano **Piovanelli** (seventy-five), archbishop of Florence, slight in build but large of heart and very much a man of dialogue, who allowed his cathedral to be used for the funeral of the controversial progressive priest Ernesto Balducci. He has shown solidarity with immigrants, inaugurated a hospice for those with AIDS, spoken out against anti-Semitism, supported ecumenism, appealed against the arms trade, and condemned corruption in Italian politics. In Florence he is a much-loved pastor, but at seventy-five he may be just too old to begin a new job in Rome as pastor of the universal Church.

Of the same age is another Italian who might otherwise be an unexciting but acceptable compromise choice, Giovanni **Saldarini**, archbishop of Turin. He is a moderate who used to work closely with Martini as his episcopal vicar and who is sufficiently in John Paul's good books to have been asked to preach the Vatican's Lenten retreat in 1994.

Cardinal Virgilio **Noè** (seventy-seven) is an old curial hand, sometime papal master of ceremonies, and now holding one of the three Vatican jobs that continue during the conclave interregnum: archpriest of the Vatican Basilica and vicar general for Vatican City. So he will be flapping around, but unlikely at his age to pick up votes.

There are now six Italian cardinals left to name. Francesco Colasuonno (seventy-four) was rewarded with a cardinal's hat in the 1998 consistory for long years in the diplomatic service, including being nuncio to Italy. Salvatore De Giorgi (sixty-nine), archbishop of Palermo, is said to be good on Mafia questions, but otherwise little known. Michele Giordano (sixty-nine), archbishop of Naples, has been accused by Italian state prosecutors of involvement in a criminal money-laundering racket. We can also eliminate the Italians Lorenzo Antonetti (seventy-seven), Dino Monduzzi (seventy-seven), and Carlo Furno (seventy-eight) as being now too old.

The Other Europeans

At the younger end of the age scale, we have the second-youngest cardinal (by eight months), Christoph **Schönborn** of Vienna (fifty-four). A very young cardinal could be an even worse risk than an old one. Someone of fifty-four might be pope for as long as thirty or forty years—a terrifying prospect. Remember that the longest pontificate in history was thirty-two years. Even though resignation is a technical option, it has not been exercised for 706 years, which means any pope would be setting a pretty big precedent. Besides, by the time a man has gotten into the habit of being pope for twenty-five years or so, he will be set in his ways and less likely, rather than more likely, to do something as bold as retiring. So it is tempting to strike Schönborn off the list of *papabili*. But this would be a great mistake.

Year by year, the name of Schönborn is heard more and more persistently as a papal candidate. At first he is named as someone who "of course" is too young this time round, but could be a good bet for the next pope. The popes of the twentieth century have all, apart from John XXIII, been in the fifty-eight to sixty-eight bracket when elected: Pius X was sixty-eight; Benedict XV, fifty-nine; Pius XI, sixty-five; Pius XII, sixty-three; Paul VI, sixty-five; John Paul I, sixty-five; and John

Paul II, fifty-eight. But the suggestion of Schönborn as pope is a seed that settles and germinates. And after a while people begin to think: Well who else is there? Of course there are more than a hundred other candidates, but once you begin to look at them there is something wrong with all of them, as we shall see: too old, too stupid, too hated, too pliable, too career-minded, too inexperienced, too weak in Italian, too dodgy on health grounds, too much associated with the old regime, too much of a break with the old regime.

Who then is Schönborn? A son of old European nobility (the third cardinal of his family) and a Dominican, he is the archbishop of Vienna, indirect successor to the great Cardinal König and direct successor to the conservative and appalling Cardinal Groër—possibly the most disastrous of all John Paul's disastrous appointments, because he was forced to resign by a spate of allegations of homosexual sex abuse. Schönborn was made auxiliary of Vienna in 1995, coming in as Groër's coadjutor and taking over five months later, at a time of serious crisis. Schönborn felt the situation was so serious that he took the extraordinarily bold step of saying that, in his view and that of all but one of the other Austrian bishops, Groër must have been guilty of the charges. But initial success in handling this tricky situation was followed by the criticism that he had failed in his attempt to control the abrasive and ultraconservative supporter of Groër, Bishop Kurt Krenn.

It would be a mistake, however, to interpret this courageous handling of a ghastly mess as a sign that Schönborn is a progressive. On the contrary, he is a conservative, but a highly intelligent one, close to Ratzinger, in fact. He does not enjoy dialogue, but he is not closed to it, as was seen by the space he allowed for the We Are Church movement, which amounted to a massive national uprising, soon developing into an international force. Schönborn's other main distinction is that he was responsible for producing the *Catechism of the Catholic Church* as its editorial secretary, coordinating the contributions of about a thousand bishops in a massive five-year program from 1987 to 1992. Whatever one thinks of the wisdom of freezing doctrine into a centralized approved version, the *Catechism* is a *tour de force.*

So Schönborn has theological strength, and at the time of writing he has been variously tipped to succeed Ratzinger as head of the Congregation for the Doctrine of the Faith or to succeed Pio Laghi as head of the Congregation for Catholic Education. He is fluent in several languages, including English, French, Italian, Spanish, and Latin. He is a handsome, lovable man, and spiritual enough to have been invited to preach the pope's Lenten retreat in 1996 (just as Cardinal Wojtyla had preached it for Paul VI). He is conservative enough to support the new movements—like the Neocatechumenate, the Legionaries of Christ, and Focolare—but he is "not a head-basher," according to his U.S. Jesuit friend Joseph Fessio. He even has the blessing of Cardinal König, who was a kingmaker when Wojtyla was elected and at ninety-four is still a voice that commands tremendous respect, particularly among progressives. When Schönborn was made a cardinal in 1998 he said, "This appointment is to be seen as more than a confirmation of power, but also as a real renewal of the Church in our country and a seeking of positive dialogue."

Given the cardinals appointed by John Paul II, only a conservative can win enough votes to become pope, but given the nature of the job, only a man of genuine talent could take it on. In the opinion of many in Rome, Schönborn has enough talent and enough integrity to sit on the chair of Peter. Could this be enough to break the barrier of his youthful age? It would be an act of faith, because he is four years younger than Wojtyla at his election. The cardinals were only prepared to go for someone so young then because John Paul I had died after only one month, and they had to open up their categories in one way or another if they were not to be reduced to accepting a second-choice pope. Would the cardinals take an even bigger risk today? They would hesitate, they would look hard for someone else, but one cardinal said privately that if Schönborn was too young for the job, that was a fault that time would heal. It might even be that the cardinals would discuss the question of papal resignation as a possible way forward in a world where good medical care leads to longer lives, and that Schönborn might express himself in favor of popes retiring, without, of course, having his own case in mind.

Such are the reasons to consider Schönborn as *papabile*, but though they make up a strong case, it is not strong enough. Despite his youthful fifty-four, Schönborn has a question mark over his health. The day before a tricky "delegates' summit" in October 1998 with representatives from both We Are Church and conservative groupings, he was rushed to hospital with a pulmonary embolism, the very problem that caused the death of John Paul I. There seems no doubt that it was stress-related. Further evidence of his inability to cope with tensions in the Church is shown by his hesitancy to make decisions, his fear of the media, and his use of the most inappropriate imagery, as when he compared a divorced person wishing to remarry to a paraplegic wishing to ride a motorbike. Schönborn may attract a rising number of votes, but those who know him better believe he may not be able to cope with the demands of the job.

Cardinal Joseph **Ratzinger** (seventy-two) is so well known that people tend to overlook him as a papal candidate. They have become so used to him as the big bad wolf of the new inquisition—technically the prefect of the Congregation for the Doctrine of the Faith—that they cannot imagine him in any other job. For some the thought is just too terrible to contemplate—that the man deemed responsible for so many of the most controversial actions of this papacy might succeed to it one day. Ratzinger has soaked up much of the odium that Catholics, still loyal at heart to their Holy Father, wish to deflect from John Paul himself. The doctrinal investigations into Hans Küng and Edward Schillebeeckx, into Ivone Gebara and Leonardo Boff, into Tissa Balasuriya and Jacques Dupuis, not to mention a host of other, less high-profile names, are all laid at the door of Ratzinger's congregation. To have him as pope would be inconceivably divisive, runs the common wisdom. Besides, people say, clutching at straws, he is too old.

He probably is too old, but if he is too old then so too is Martini, who is two months his senior. Ratzinger has had health problems in the last five years, and it is understood he has been trying to retire from the CDF. That is probably enough to tip the balance. But apart from that, the case that can be made for him becoming pope is very strong indeed. He is, after all, so outstanding in his own way that Cardinal Oddi made a public appeal for his candidacy in 1996. Oddi's only reservation, he said, was that there was a general practice of "following a fat pope with a lean one," that is to say, of going for someone completely different. Ratzinger has been such a close collaborator with John Paul that he would not appear as a new face.

In favor of Ratzinger is that he is a man of outstanding ability and intelligence. Now associated with the most conservative positions doctrinally—he interprets his job as the strict policing of orthodoxy—he has not always been seen that way. On the contrary, he was one of the most creative, brilliant, and respected theologians of Germany, which has long enjoyed a theological preeminence among the nations; he taught dogmatics in the most famous German universi-ties—Münster, Tübingen, Regensburg—and was one of Paul VI's choices both as bishop and as cardinal. His appointment to the CDF, early in John Paul's pontificate, initially seemed an enlightened move.

Given the makeup of the college of cardinals, only a conservative can plausibly gain enough votes. But most conservatives appear second-raters, if not third-raters, after John Paul II, who, whatever his faults, is indisputably a man of outstanding talent. Ratzinger is the only conservative in the college of electors who can stand shoulder to shoulder with Wojtyla in terms of natural ability. He would exercise continuity of policy, but without being a pale reflection of his predecessor. He would establish his own style and has the experience and confidence to be able to carry off what is one of the most demanding jobs in the world. He has all the language skills needed for the job, yet would continue the precedent of appointing a non-Italian. He would be in charge of the Curia, rather than the Curia in charge of him.

Second, Ratzinger makes a very good impression on those who meet him. He may have a reputation for being an ogre, but he comes across as charming and personable, courteous and even spiritual, with his Bavarian smile and love of Mozart. He could overcome his terrible image within the first ten minutes of appearing on television as the new pope. There would be a legacy of mistrust, but nothing that could not be overcome by the perpetual hopefulness of the great majority of the People of God, who long to believe in and love their pope. Every September Ratzinger meets his former doctoral students somewhere in the Alps, halfway between Italy and Germany, and for a week's holiday they engage with him on a basis of approximate theological equality, considering him someone who shares with them a common spiritual endeavor. Bishops who have had interviews with Ratzinger tend to be much more positive than those who judge him only by what he has done. One progressive cardinal said privately, "I would rather have Ratzinger than many other conservatives I could mention."

Another powerful curial cardinal who is not Italian is Cardinal Jan Pieter **Schotte** of Belgium (seventy-one). He has been secretary-general of the Synod of Bishops since 1985 and is one of the most powerful men in Rome. He is a highly capable organizer and speaks six languages. More than that, he is a manipulator and has learned how to make the synods work efficiently by appointing a secret team of behind-the-scenes drafters for the documents: their names are hidden among a long list of supposed *periti,* or theological experts, the great majority of whom have nothing to do. Schotte has been responsible for the excessive and ever increasing level of secrecy that surrounds the operations of the various synods. Journalists are allowed in—strictly supervised—to hear the bishops saying their morning prayers, but after that they are expelled. Nearly all the synod working documents, even the final propositions, are branded *"sub secreto."* The propositions have to be handed back in, so even the bishops cannot take them home unless they make an illegal photocopy. And the time available for doing that has been reduced: bishops used to be allowed to look at them overnight, to decide how to vote, but at the 1998 Synod for Oceania and the 1999 European Synod they could keep them only over the lunch break.

Bishops used to be allowed to release their speeches to the press, if they chose to do so, but since 1998 even that has been banned. Schotte has even forbidden the guardian of orthodoxy, Cardinal Ratzinger, to publish his speeches inside the synod. Great show is made of the fact that elections for the postsynod council are democratic, with strips of cellophane tape sealing the boxes in the sight of all the synod fathers; yet outside in the corridors Schotte could be overheard discussing with a colleague how to replace one elected representative with another who came second. "It is quite simple," Schotte was alleged to have said, "we simply ask the first man to stand down." Schotte was also overheard at a papal lunch complaining to John Paul II about that Margaret Hebblethwaite woman who was trying to find out what was going on inside the synod. He will be a kingmaker, because he knows just how to work the system, but is unlikely to be elected pope himself, because people do not like him.

Another curial cardinal whose name has been mentioned in relation to the papacy is Roger **Etchegaray** (seventy-seven), a French Basque with a gleam of silver fillings when he smiles. He used to run the Pontifical Council for Justice and Peace and is now president of the Committee for the Grand Jubilee of the Year 2000. He has acted as the pope's troubleshooter for the Mediterranean area and has made frequent visits to the former Yugoslavia in a rather desperate attempt to maintain good relations with the Muslims (relative success) and the Serbian Orthodox (relative failure). Previously archbishop of Marseilles, he has an outlook that embraces the whole Mediterranean area, and his great boast is that he founded the CCEE (Council of European Episcopal Conferences). But at seventy-seven his chances are now remote.

French Cardinal Paul **Poupard** (sixty-nine) is a dapper, ambitious French intellectual and an old Vatican hand who has the advantage of knowing the system and speaking the languages without actually being Italian. He served in the Secretariat of State in the pontificate of Paul VI, returning to France as rector of the Institut Catholique, until he was invited to work at the Pontifical Council for Dialogue with Nonbelievers by John Paul just after his visit to Paris in 1980. In 1982 he was asked to set up the Pontifical Council for Culture, of which he is president. Since 1993, it has incorporated the former body for dialogue with unbelievers. He is the author of a big dictionary of religions and took the inspiration for his motto from St. Augustine: "I am a bishop for you, but first of all I am a Christian with you." He is said to consider himself *papabile*, which probably means he will not be.

Moving now outside the Curia, we come to another Frenchman, Cardinal Jean-Marie **Lustiger** (seventy-three), archbishop of Paris. He is a clever man, and perhaps worth a second thought as pope. The most important thing about him is that he is of Polish-Jewish origin and that he had relatives who perished at Auschwitz. A Jewish joke asks, "What is the difference between the chief rabbi of France and Cardinal Lustiger?" The answer is that "Cardinal Lustiger speaks Yiddish," which draws attention to his Polish connections. His Jewish background would not do him any harm.

But his drawback is that he seems to be entirely a creature of Pope John Paul II, who made him bishop of Orleans in 1979 and archbishop of Paris in 1981. Whether cause or consequence, Lustiger hews close to the papal line. He removed his seminarians from the Institut Catholique in Paris, deeming its theology too "speculative." He sent them instead to the Séminaire St. Paul in Louvain-la-Neuve, the Jesuit Institut d'Études Théologiques in Brussels, or the interdiocesan seminary at Issy-les-Moulineaux—all considered "sounder."

Lustiger is quite consciously trying to form Tridentine priests, men who are essentially set apart for prayer and the sacraments. "He wants," said Belgian Dominican Philippe Denis, "to be the Monsieur Olier of the twentieth century." On this seventeenth-century model, the priest is *defined* by prayer and the sacraments rather than by mission, by his relationship to God and the hierarchy rather than by his relationship to the People of God.

Lustiger admires the French seventeenth century as "a period of astonishing mysticism." It was indeed. But the effect was to transform the image of Christ the Good Shepherd into Christ the contemplator of the Father. It becomes difficult to see how pastoral and missionary-minded priests can emerge from this process. Lustiger could be considered the candidate of the "charismatic" movement, especially in its French form, the Emmanuel community. He has given their priests charge of the parish of La Trinité, in the ninth arrondissement. Their otherworldly spirit is summed up in their statutes: "To be the brother of Jesus, one must have the Heart of Jesus; and for that one must take Mary into one's household and let the Holy Spirit renew our hearts."

Glasgow's Cardinal Thomas **Winning** (seventy-four) presents himself as a plain, blunt man and has a certain appeal in that role. His style is about as different as could be from that of the late Cardinal Basil Hume in Westminster. Where Hume was the English gentleman of stature who spoke with prudence, Winning is the common man, from a large Scots-Irish family, who does not mince his words and has an openly socialist and antiwar approach to political issues. He has plenty of vision: he developed an ambitious pastoral restructuring for his archdiocese, ran up a massive debt, and before he had paid it off, still had the energy to launch an ambitious program to give financial help to young mothers tempted by abortion. Though he is essentially a domestic man rather than an internationalist, he is competent in Italian, having been spiritual director at the Scots college in Rome for three years. The Scottish press became excited at the thought of Winning for pope, after he made some fairly obvious and unexceptional remarks to give a sense of proportion to the Church's teaching against contraception: they hailed him as a man with the sort of wisdom and prudence to rescue the Church from an embarrassing position.

But like so many of the other possible contenders, he is just too old for the job.

Still in his sixties is a Belgian with a broader outlook and a stronger theological foundation, Cardinal Godfried **Danneels** (sixty-six). His name has been associated with Martini and with Hume, when he was alive, for he comes from the more liberal background of those inspired by Vatican II. He is one of the few cardinals with vision and clear analysis, but he is not particularly inspiring. He can make a good speech and has done so as president of Pax Christi, but he only comes alive when he is on a platform. He is said to lack human warmth and, as professor of liturgy at the Catholic University of Leuven, to have had the reputation of being a loner who did not communicate with the rest of the faculty. So, sadly for Belgium, which has produced so many fine theologians, he will probably be passed over.

Cardinal Adrianus Johannes **Simonis** (sixty-nine) was appointed by John Paul II, first as coadjutor and then as archbishop of Utrecht, to sort out the Dutch Church. Now that Holland is slowly moving toward more dialogue, he has the air of a man on the way out. Cardinal Henri **Schwery** (sixty-seven) of Sion, Switzerland, was an unusual choice for cardinal, for the Swiss bishops are so democratic that they have neither primate nor even archbishops, and the presidency rotates; in any case he has now retired from Sion for health reasons, so is not a candidate for a more important job. Moving on to Germany, we find Cardinal Joachim **Meisner** (sixty-six), who was nominated by John Paul to be archbishop of Cologne despite the fact that he was not on the list drawn up, according to tradition, by the cathedral chapter, but was parachuted in from East Berlin. Cardinal Friedrich **Wetter** (seventy-one), archbishop of München und Freising, occupies Ratzinger's old diocese. Cardinal Georg Maximilian **Sterzinsky** (sixty-three), has been archbishop of Berlin since May 1989 and so has seen his church through a dramatic time of change.

We met Cardinal Eduardo **Martínez Somalo** (seventy-two), the pope's *camerlengo* or chamberlain, on the first page of Chapter 1. He is a Spanish traditionalist of dull, pious appearance, who has become one of the group of Spanish-speaking Vatican conservatives, together with Medina Estévez, López Trujillo, and Sodano (former nuncio to Chile), who worked behind the scenes to have Pinochet released from his arrest in Britain. He has a background in canon law and diplomatic experience in Britain and Colombia, before moving to the Vatican in 1979, where he was briefly substitute, or *sostituto*, and became one of the pope's closest aides. He is now prefect of the Congregation for Institutes of Consecrated Life and for Societies of Apostolic Life. A "friend of Opus Dei," he is devoid of vision and likely to join in the Stop Martini movement.

Two more Spaniards must be considered. Ricardo María **Carles Gordó** (seventy-three), archbishop of Barcelona, is an intelligent conservative, yet less so than Antonio María **Rouco Varela** (sixty-three), archbishop of Madrid, who is much the more *papabile* of the two. Both are canon lawyers. Carles was elected vice-president of the Spanish Episcopal Conference in March 1999, but Rouco Varela became the president. Carles was in favor of the bishops making some kind of premillennial "gesture of reconciliation" in acknowledgment of the Church's support for General Franco, but Rouco Varela thought it inappropriate.

Rouco Varela is a man with a long nose and big glasses. He was archbishop of the pilgrimage center Santiago de Compostela for ten years before going on to Madrid in 1994. John Paul took to him when he organized a big youth event at Santiago with lots of rousing music, and then took Varela with him (as well as Carles) on his trip to Cuba. He is spoken of within Spain as a runner for the papacy, and he is a better age for the job than Carles. When the suggestion was put to him, Rouco Varela replied, "Any man of the Christian faithful can be elected pope." Carles's comment about Rouco Varela as papal candidate was, "Often he who goes into the conclave as pope comes out as cardinal." Rouco Varela was *relator* at the Second Synod for Europe in October of 1999, but his deeply pessimistic presentation of contemporary culture was generally thought to damage his chances of the papacy. Yet he is a good linguist and an elegant, incisive writer. He has an enormous capacity for work and has very many admirers. If the papacy does not go to an Italian, and if the cardinals cannot agree on a Latin American, Rouco Varela cannot be ruled out.

The remaining Spanish cardinal, Antonio Maria Javierre **Ortas** (seventy-eight), former prefect of the Congregation for Divine Worship and the Discipline of the Sacraments, must be considered too old.

North of the Pyrenees, we come to the cardinal archbishop of Bordeaux, Pierre **Eyt** (sixty-five), who is interested in peace issues and is a suitable age. A moderate but rigorous theologian (he attacked the German progressive theologian Eugen Drewermann), he is said to be pastorally warm, and he made an excellent impression at the Second Synod for Europe. But he lacks the international profile to pull many votes and also the fluency in different languages that he would need as pope. The Swiss Gilberto **Agustoni** (seventy-seven) is now too old. The Lebanese Nasrallah Pierre **Sfeir** (seventy-nine) is even older.

Moving to Eastern Europe, there is one cardinal who stands out, Miloslav **Vlk** (sixty-seven) from the Czech Republic. His name means "wolf," and he is the son of an unmarried mother, though his mother married his father, a farmer, when he was six. The young Miloslav worked as a cowherd as a child, and as a window-cleaner under the Communists. John Paul II arranged for him, now archbishop of Prague, to oust Martini as president of the CCEE by a simple rule change: instead of *electing* a special representative to the CCEE, chosen on grounds, for example, of linguistic competence, episcopal conferences would send their presidents as *ipso facto* delegates. He has a certain presence, but nothing like the charisma of Wojtyla, nor the brains, nor the versatility, nor the vision, and certainly not the languages. Even his Italian is a little shaky, though his German is fine. To choose another Eastern European is to invite comparison with his predecessor, and Vlk could only come off the worse for that. But he is an attractive figure, authoritative but not pushy, conservative but not militant. He is influenced by the Focolare movement, with its rather uncritical tradition of lay spirituality, and he helped to smuggle Focolare literature into Czechoslovakia in the 1960s.

Then there is the Slovak Jozef **Tomko** (seventy-five), prefect of the Congregation for the Evangelization of Peoples (previously known as Propaganda Fide until Dr. Joseph Goebbels made the term useless). He bases his position on the fact that Slovakia, now an independent nation, never had an imperialist past. (The same claim was made by his predecessor, Dermot Ryan, former archbishop of Dublin.) Maybe, but Tomko's previous experience in the Congregation for the Doctrine of the Faith suggests that he is essentially an inquisitor. He may well bustle about as a kingmaker during the conclave, but we can probably count him out of the running himself, on age grounds.

Jesuit Jan Chryzostom **Korec** (seventy-five), who has seen the inside of a Communist jail, was secretly consecrated bishop in 1951 only a year after his priestly ordination. He became bishop of Nitra, Slovakia, in 1990. He may pick up some East European votes.

Vinko **Puljic** of Sarajevo (fifty-four), the youngest cardinal, who got to know the pope during the preparations for the visit to Bosnia that had to be postponed and who made a good impression at the European Synod of 1999, is still too young for the job, not having Schönborn's outstanding brilliance and established, international reputation. Cardinal Laszlo **Paskai** (seventy-two) is archbishop of Esztergom-Budapest, primate of Hungary, and a Franciscan. He was made bishop by Paul VI and cardinal by John Paul II back in 1988. His contribution to the Synod on Consecrated Life was to say that obedience had been corrupted by democratic sentiments. The Lithuanian Vincentas Sladkevicius (seventy-nine) is almost eighty.

Of the Europeans, that now leaves only the archbishop of Warsaw, Józef **Glemp** (seventy); the archbishop of Wroclaw, Henryk Roman **Gulbinowicz** (seventy-one); the archbishop of Kraków, Franciszek **Macharski** (seventy-two); and the retired president of the Pontifical Council for Social Communications, Andrzej Maria **Deskur** (seventy-five), who as Poles can be more decisively ruled out than anyone else.

The North Americans

But Europe is not the Church; indeed there are now many appeals for a truly international Church to avoid Eurocentrism. North America consists of more than the United States, but it is the United States that is particularly rich in cardinals. Unfortunately the country suffers from the stigma of being a superpower. A pope from the United States would seem even more associated with neocolonial domination than a pope from the old colonial countries of Europe. What is more, with all the distrust of unbridled capitalism, valueless secularism, and indiscriminate feminism that has festered during this papacy, a pope from the United States would seem a very dodgy proposition. He would be regarded, on the one hand, as a further extension of excessive control by the world's only remaining superpower and, on the other, as tainted by association with dangerous cultural values. The United States must be regarded, to all intents and purposes, as blackballed when it comes to the matter of electing a pope. That will not stop us, however, from enjoying the fun of thinking "what if."

If there were one U.S. cardinal who could be considered *papabile*, it would be Cardinal Roger **Mahony** (sixty-three), archbishop of Los Angeles. He runs a large and important diocese of 4.5 million Catholics, a very multicultural city, and the Asian capital of the United States. And he straddles the boundary of North America and Latin America in the sense that he is a Spanish speaker: he learned it by working alongside Mexican workers on his father's poultry farm. His father was a "full-blooded Canadian Italian" from Vancouver, and he owes his Irish name to the Irish family who adopted him; his mother, Loretta Marie Baron, was a German American from Ohio. When installed as archbishop in St. Vibiana's Cathedral (now demolished), Mahony greeted his multiracial diocese not only in English and Spanish, but in Vietnamese and Hungarian. He is genuinely popular, he commands trust, and he can be fun to be with. Though he has suffered from prostate cancer, he was given a clean bill of health after treatment.

He reads serious theology and has a sense of what Rome is about. In his former classmate Archbishop Justin Rigali, secretary of the Congregation for Bishops, he had a hot line to Rome until early in 1994, when Rigali became archbishop of St. Louis. Mahony is himself a member of a couple of Vatican dicasteries. He was also a copresident of the Synod for America.

And he can be tough. When Mother Angelica of television fame accused him in 1997 of denying the real presence of

Christ in the Eucharist and called on the Catholics of his diocese to practice zero obedience, Mahony demanded an apology. He received one, but only alongside a repeated complaint that his pastoral letter on the Eucharist had been unclear on Church teaching. He then reported her to the Congregation for Institutes of Consecrated Life and to the Pontifical Council for Social Communications, saying she had breached canon 753 (the faithful are bound to adhere to the magisterium of their bishops, the authentic teachers of the faith) and canon 1373 (someone who provokes subjects to disobedience is to be punished by interdict or other just penalties).

In fact Mahony has only one drawback: he comes from the superpower United States. He was even born in glossy, legendary Hollywood, together with his twin brother, Louis. When he arrived as archbishop in Los Angeles in 1985, it was said that he was suffering from two kinds of fever: scarlet fever (for the cardinal's red biretta) and white fever (for the papacy), but he denies that he is "a man who would be pope." He can see the problems with any U.S. citizen being considered in the foreseeable future.[2]

The U.S. cardinal currently developing a Vatican career is James **Stafford** (sixty-seven), president of the Pontifical Council for the Laity and a protégé of Ratzinger, being a member of the Congregation for the Doctrine of the Faith. He has a strong background in various ecumenical dialogues: Catholic-Orthodox, Catholic-Lutheran, and Catholic-Jewish. He has helped organize World Youth Days, both in 1993 and 1997, and headed the U.S. Catholic Conference on Marriage and Family Life for six years, which earned him a place at the 1980 Synod on the Role of the Christian Family—his first visit to Rome. He may look on paper as though he has good experience, but he is not much liked.

The other two U.S. cardinals working in the Vatican are over seventy, which adds an age disadvantage to the already massive impediment of coming from the United States. William Wakefield **Baum** (seventy-three), former bishop of Washington, heads the Apostolic Penitentiary, but is very ill; he is the only U.S. cardinal ever to have voted in a conclave—in fact two—having become a cardinal in 1976. Cardinal Edmund **Szoka** (seventy-two), former archbishop of Detroit, has been in Rome since 1990 and now oversees the civil government of the Vatican as president of the Pontifical Commission for the Vatican City State, a job he took on at the geriatric age of seventy.

Cardinal Archbishop Francis **George** (sixty-two), an Oblate of Mary Immaculate, has stepped into the ministry so brilliantly exercised by the late Cardinal Bernardin in the second largest U.S. diocese, Chicago. Short and bald, he wears a leg brace and limps, having suffered from polio when he was thirteen, but this disability may count more in his favor than against him. He is clever—a former professor of philosophy—and articulate—he even speaks four languages. He could go far, but is still too much of a new boy to have made his name much known with the other cardinals.

Cardinal William **Keeler** (sixty-eight), archbishop of Baltimore, was a *peritus* at Vatican II, but he now believes U.S. Catholics have been misled by a false interpretation of the council. He is worried about the upbringing of young people by parents who have an inadequate grounding in the faith and advocates more attention to the catechism. He has been involved in dialogue with Jews, but maintains a high view of the papacy. His views might be acceptable to many of the cardinals, but he is man who looks backward rather than forward, and, again, his nationality is the fatal stumbling block.

Cardinal Archbishop Bernard **Law** of Boston (sixty-eight) is an affable man. He was educated at Harvard, but has a simple piety, admiring St. Charles Borromeo and Mother Teresa of Calcutta. Archbishop Adam **Maida** of

Detroit (sixty-nine), whose parents came from Poland, is a cardinal lacking in star quality, but has his own type of ambition, such as building a John Paul II Center at Catholic University, Washington.

The cardinals nearing eighty are much too old for serious consideration for the papacy, especially coming from the United States: James Aloysius **Hickey** (seventy-nine), the cardinal archbishop of Washington, and John Joseph **O'Connor** (seventy-nine), the cardinal archbishop of New York. Cardinal Anthony Joseph **Bevilacqua** (seventy-six), archbishop of Philadelphia, is not much younger.

Canada, however, is not under suspicion in quite the way that the United State is, and so we can take a more serious look at the Canadian candidates, of which there are two under eighty. The cardinal archbishop of Montreal, Jean-Claude **Turcotte** (sixty-three), could be a real possibility. Not only is he the right age, but he was the only bishop at the Synod for America to be elected to the postsynodal council on the first ballot. Being a French Canadian is definitely a plus over being an English Canadian, because it makes him part of a minority, and one minority can understand the problems of another. Turcotte shows some evidence that this is the case: in 1998 he allowed thirty Chileans seeking refugee status to stay in St. Jean de la Croix church when they were afraid of deportation. He has a background of ministry to the Young Christian Workers' movement, is an active proponent of the Church's social doctrine, and feels particularly strongly about unemployment. He has simple tastes and a common touch. He is shaped by Vatican II in his thinking: in his opinion, "the Church has not yet completely digested the Council." He believes in the move from a hierarchically based Church to the "People of God."

The other Canadian is Cardinal Aloysius **Ambrozic** (sixty-nine), archbishop of Toronto. Born in Slovenia, then part of Yugoslavia, he came to Canada after the World War II at the age of eighteen. He studied in Rome and Wurzburg, Germany, and is a New Testament scholar. He has only been a cardinal since 1998 and is unlikely to be known well enough to attract votes.

The Latin Americans

If the Italians are to let go of the papacy for the second time running, without it being prized from their unwilling fingers, then a Latin American is the next best thing to an Italian. Spanish is close to Italian as a language, and the Spanish-speaking world is a huge chunk of well-tested Catholicism with a centuries-long pedigree. Spanish speakers can be trusted to come from a properly Catholic culture and to be neither polluted by extraneous cultural influences, nor nervous to establish their credentials by adhering to the rule book. There is a sense among Italian *vaticanisti*, who tend to think they are the only reliable experts on the Vatican, that a Latin American could be acceptable.

Barely out of North America, we find another three cardinals in Mexico. The most clearly *papabile* is the cardinal archbishop of Mexico City, Norberto **Rivera Carrera** (fifty-seven), who manages a diocese of nearly 19 million people that includes the famous pilgrimage site of Our Lady of Guadalupe, the image imprinted miraculously (so it is said) on the cloak of an indigenous peasant, Juan Diego, in 1531. It was Cardinal Rivera's initiative at the Synod for America to appeal to John Paul II to visit Guadalupe for the publication of the postsynodal exhortation: the suggestion drew spontaneous applause, and it was followed. He drew more applause at the synod when he called for the canonization of Juan Diego (whom some scholars regard as a historically dubious figure), and Rivera was quickly elected moderator of his discussion group. He has a concern for social issues, promoting work cooperatives, condemning disregard for human rights, and describing the international debt hanging over Mexico as a form of "bloodletting." He has been called *papabile* partly because he received some prominence during the January 1999 papal visit to Mexico City and partly because he is believed to be the candidate favored by the Legionaries of Christ, a recent, flourishing, conservative congregation of priests. He has only, however, been a cardinal since 1998, so he is still finding his feet, and at fifty-seven he would be even younger than John Paul II at his election. A cardinal in his sixties would be preferable.

The other Mexican contenders have been cardinals since 1994: Juan **Sandoval Iñiguez** (sixty-six), archbishop of Guadalajara, comes from a devout Catholic family with twelve children. Though generally rigidly conservative, he is a convinced critic of unbridled capitalism for the way it makes the rich richer and the poor poorer. Despite his conservatism, he demanded an inquiry into the assassination of his predecessor, Cardinal Posadas Ocampo, in May 1993, against the wishes of both the government and the nuncio. His background is in seminary formation, first as spiritual director and then as rector. He got a good showing in Rome when he was *relator* at the Synod for America.

Cardinal Adolfo Antonio **Suárez Rivera** (seventy-two), archbishop of Monterrey, also feels strongly about international debt. He is a widely respected man of principle, and has even been compared to Oscar Romero in the sense that he is a conservative who could show great courage. When he was president of the Mexican bishops' conference, he resisted attempts by the papal nuncio to dominate its agenda.

Cardinal Miguel **Obando Bravo** (seventy-three), archbishop of Managua, has long gained a name for himself by his pugnacious resistance to the Sandinistas. He has been a cardinal since 1985, but has been a bishop for more than thirty years, ever since 1968, the year of *Humane Vitae*. He opposed the dictatorship of Somoza as well, so he is something of a fighter, and he even continues to exercise some political influence in the increasingly corrupt regime of President Alemán. He has built a new and hideous cathedral, covered in little concrete domes, with a donation from a U.S. pizza magnate. It feels very difficult to imagine him outside Nicaragua.

Moving east from Central America, we come to Cuba, with its equally well known Cardinal Jaime Lucas **Ortega y Alamino** (sixty-three). Like Obando Bravo, he has been a thorn in the side of the political regime, but he is ten years younger. He spent 1967 in detention, which always adds to the respect a bishop can command. He chose a pelican for his coat of arms, which in legend wounds its breast to feed its young on its own blood and in iconography is a figure of Christ. He says he feels "very close to the pontificate of John Paul II." It may be only lack of imagination that makes him seem inseparable from Cuba, but the electors might think another cardinal from a Communist country would be too repetitious.

Farther east we come to the Dominican Republic and Cardinal Nicolás de Jesús **López Rodríguez** (sixty-three), who was host to the last Latin American bishops' meeting in Santo Domingo in September 1992, a year after he became cardinal and eleven years after he became archbishop of Santo Domingo. He was also, at the time, president of CELAM (*Consejo Episcopal Latinoamericano*, or Latin-American Bishops' Council), who organized the celebrations for the 500th anniversary of Christopher Columbus's arrival in the Americas. The conference was designed as a rally in support of conservative positions, and the conservative position, in this context, meant declaring that the five centuries were grounds for unmixed rejoicing. This was certainly the view of Cardinal López Rodríguez, and the event was to be marked by the building of a huge mausoleum designed to house what the Dominican Republic claimed were the bones of Columbus and compared by some visitors to a multistory parking garage or an Aztec temple.[3]

Brazilians like Cardinal Arns and Cardinal Lorscheider detested the monument because it represented that alliance of Church and state rejected by most of the Latin American bishops, and even more because over a thousand families had to be evicted from the site to make space for it. But Cardinal López Rodríguez called critics in the local press "loud-mouths and layabouts." Those who said the Church had something to repent for as well as to celebrate were dismissed as suffering from "a guilt complex that will lessen zeal for the new evangelization."[4] Just to the east of the Dominican Republic we come to Puerto Rico and Cardinal Luis Aponte Martínez (seventy-seven), who must now be considered too old to be pope.

Cardinal López Rodríguez of Santo Domingo is not to be confused with Cardinal Alfonso **López Trujillo** (sixty-four) of Colombia, who works in the Vatican and is president of the Pontifical Council for the Family. He is believed to consider himself a very strong candidate for the papacy, and in terms of paper qualifications he is indeed hard to match. Right age, right continent, decades of international experience—he was secretary-general of CELAM at the age of thirty-seven and went on to become its president, has been a cardinal since 1983, and has held his job in Rome since 1990. And being conservative cannot be seen as a drawback when nearly all the electors are conservatives. However, it is probably safe to say his chances are remote. He lacks one crucial quality, and that quality is holiness. López Trujillo is probably the most sinister man in Rome. He wears dark glasses and padded shoulders and has a mafioso-like appearance; it is widely believed he knows more about the Colombian drug trade than a cardinal should. It is hard to find anyone who has a good word to say about him. He is also a purgatorially boring speaker.

López Trujillo must be attended to if only because his rise has been so meteoric. He began to show his true nature when preparing for Puebla—the Latin American bishops' meeting in 1979, before Santo Domingo. In his mind the purpose of Puebla was to reverse the decisions of Medellín, the famous meeting in 1968, before Puebla, which had given a huge boost to liberation theology throughout the whole of Latin America. He said on a tape that by chance fell into the hands of a journalist, "I am convinced that people like Arrupe and Pironio ... must be told to their faces that they must change their attitude."[5] Pedro Arrupe, the late General of the Jesuits, and Eduardo Pironio, the late Argentinian cardinal who was president of CELAM at the time of that great Medellín meeting, were two of the finest men in the Church at that time, of a quality that is rarely found today.

In the early 1980s, when he was beginning to look like a papal contender, he was close to Cardinal Sebastiano Baggio, then prefect of the Congregation for Bishops and the sworn enemy of "base communities" and "liberation theology." Ambitious and unscrupulous, he used an eccentric Belgian, Roger Vekemans, who by this time had more contacts with the CIA than with the Society of Jesus, to which he ostensibly belonged. Through the Agency for International Development (AID), a front for the CIA, he channeled over $5 million into anti–liberation theology projects. They also had access to Adveniat funds administered by Franz Hengsbach, bishop of Essen, in Germany.

Writing to a Brazilian reactionary, Archbishop Luciano Cabral Duarte, López Trujillo rejoiced in the election of Pope John Paul II because he had spoken "very clearly against the deviations" of liberation theology. He prepared for battle: "Prepare your bomber planes," he wrote, "you must start training the way boxers do before going into the ring for a world championship. May your blows be evangelical and sure." After that, he was revealed and ceased to be considered as a religious figure. He quarreled with Pax Christi over a report on Central America. In Medellín, where he was archbishop, he turned the old downtown seminary into a commercial center, its beautiful barrel-vaulted chapel becoming the restaurant. These connections and revelations would have destroyed a less well connected man, but López Trujillo enjoyed the favor of Pope John Paul II, who brought him to Rome in 1990 as president of the Pontifical Council for the Family.

He is not the only Colombian cardinal to be *papabile.* There is also Darío **Castrillón Hoyos,** who is older in years (he is seventy), but has been a cardinal only since 1998. Castrillón is beginning to look very plausible. He is mindblowingly conservative on Church matters: no speaker at synods has been able to project a more clericalist view of the priest or to produce a more depressing list of complaints about secular dress, scandal to the simple faithful, and the dangers of false propheticism, irenicism, and syncretism. He can sound like a parody of a conservative bishop, so extreme are his attitudes on Church affairs. Nor does he even have the merit of being fiery; he sounds rather dull. Yet at the same time he has strong qualities. Where López Trujillo is a careerist, Castrillón is a man of courage. Where López Trujillo is unscrupulous, Castrillón is conscientious. But he is a man of his period, of the preconciliar generation.

Ever since the Colombian novelist Gabriel García Márquez published an interview hailing him as a possible pope, the world has known (or at least the readers of the *Guardian,* April 24, 1999, have known) that Castrillón is a man to watch. "This rustic man with the profile of an eagle," he called him, the "cardinal who humbled a drug baron." But the Italian *vaticanisti* had already been following him as a *papabile*, ever since he was copresident at the December 1997 Synod for America, before he ever was a cardinal. By that time he had already been both secretary-general and president of CELAM (1983–91) and archbishop of Bucaramanga (1992–96) and was working in Rome as prefect of the Congregation for the Clergy, a post he still holds.

Quietly working away to do good, Castrillón used not only to advise the poor to be diligent, but tell the rich to distribute their wealth. He confronted coffee barons with their greed and corruption and went, dressed as a milkman, to the house of the drug baron Pablo Escobar to challenge him to confess his sins. He did. Castrillón would trudge long hours through the jungle to mediate for both with left-wing guerrillas and right-wing paramilitaries. He would walk the streets at night to feed the street children, and when he found them shot, he went to the chief of police. "Answer me," he demanded. "Where are my children?" He appealed to George Bush to end the U.S. economic embargo when the Sandinistas were in power in Nicaragua, and he believes that Marxism will be a temptation so long as the vast gulf between rich and poor remains. But, far from sympathizing with liberation theology, he criticizes priests who "reduce their ministry to social work," who are "laicized in their thinking and way of dressing," or who "no longer understand sacred celibacy." He blasted the five-year pastoral program produced by the Latin American Confederation of Religious, "Word-life," maintaining that it explained the Bible "in a way that does not agree with Catholic teaching." His combination of courage and blindness is a baffling one, and everything depends on which way the other cardinals read him.

Moving on to the Brazilians, we come to Cardinal Lucas **Moreira Neves** (seventy-four), a conservative who is very well known and highly qualified by his international experience. He spent long years in Rome at the Congregation for Bishops, first as secretary, and now—after a spell back in Brazil as archbishop of Salvador and president of the Brazilian bishops' conference, or CNBB—as prefect of the same Roman congregation. Few can have borne more responsibility than he for the run of unenlightened conservative bishops since the death of Paul VI, changing the face of the Church in a way that will take decades to reverse. Yet he diplomatically deflects the criticism, rejecting the classification of "conservative," because "labels are good for bottles, or insects, not for people."

Moreira Neves is no battle-ax, but a courteous, decent, modest, and rather spiritual man. A few years ago he looked so strongly *papabile* that it was said he was John Paul's own candidate for the succession. But he denies this strongly. "It is pure speculation," he was saying in 1996. "I know it circulates at an international level, but it has no basis and I do not pay it the slightest attention." Today it is not just his advancing age but his poor health that is the question mark. He is a diabetic, and though he insists his health is stable, there are alarming stories of how he has had to be taken off airplanes to receive medical help. Although the cardinal electors will be very cautious of electing another pope, after John Paul I, with health problems, Moreira Neves must remain on the short list, though no longer near the top of it. He is conservative, but not militant; holy, but not ineffectually pious; capable, but not a mere bureaucrat; smooth, but never oily. He is skilled in languages (he studied in France and speaks fluent Spanish and Italian as well as his native Portuguese), but would project a different image from John Paul II's. For a start, he is small and slight in build, with just a faint hint of

Negro features discernible in his olive skin (his maternal grandfather was black). He is no colossus, but a charming, modest man who never puts a foot wrong.

Already mentioned are the two great Brazilians we first met in Chapter 3, both of whom are now over seventy-five and certainly (but sadly) out of the running: Aloísio **Lorscheider** (seventy-five), a famous bishop of a liberationist outlook, and his fellow Franciscan, Brazil's greatest cardinal of our days, Paulo Evaristo **Arns** of São Paulo (seventy-eight). Arns was very much a Paul VI man: when he used to visit him in Rome, Arns recounted, the pope would "get up from his chair, embrace me, take me by the arm and begin to walk around the room. He would go as far as the window and talk about his plans. He used to speak as a true colleague." Arns, with his determined and imaginative advocacy for the poor, his pioneering development of base communities, and his courageous stand on human rights, has long been seen as a loose canon by Rome, and his resignation offered at seventy-five was promptly accepted. His age and ill health now mean the Curia has nothing to fear from him. Both Franciscans have been browbeaten in this papacy, and their contribution is over.

The ultraconservative archbishop of Rio de Janeiro, Eugênio de Araújo Sales (seventy-nine), is also much too old. So too, probably, is Serafim Fernandes de Araújo (seventy-five) archbishop of Belo Horizonte. Not much younger is Cardinal José Freire **Falcão** (seventy-four), archbishop of Brasília and an enemy of liberation theology. He is not much known outside the country and lacks a following.

Chile provides us with another curial cardinal, Jorge Arturo **Medina Estévez** (seventy-three), who is prefect of the Congregation for Divine Worship and the Discipline of the Sacraments. Very much a conservative, and a great disappointment after the great Chilean cardinal Raúl Silva Henríquez, who died in 1999, Medina Estévez has been much concerned with toning down inclusive language in the English lectionary; before that he worked on the commission preparing the new Code of Canon Law and has been a member of the International Theological Commission. In short, he has moved in all the right circles and has even given the papal retreat—that special mark of papal favor. He has spoken out against allowing dispensations to priests who want to be laicized until they are forty years old—"Sometimes a priest initially thinks about leaving the ministry, but later becomes aware that this was a transitory phase"—and against allowing the divorced and remarried to receive the sacraments—"It would be inconsistent to seek to participate in eucharistic communion while one's practical life shows a rejection of God's law." If he becomes pope, God help us.

The Venezuelan (former curial cardinal) Rosalio José Castillo Lara (seventy-seven) and the Peruvian Augusto Vargas Alzamora (seventy-seven) are surely too old.

The Africans

The leading African candidate is Cardinal Francis **Arinze** (sixty-seven) of Nigeria, the president since 1985 of the Pontifical Council for Interreligious Dialogue. He has been discussed as seriously *papabile* ever since the Hebblethwaite article in the *National Catholic Reporter* first suggested him in 1992. He sat on the papal chair during the final Mass of the Synod for Africa, when John Paul was taken to hospital with a broken femur—perhaps a sign of things to come? He was the youngest metropolitan in the world when installed as archbishop of Onitsha at the age of thirty-four. He is an outgoing and relaxed man, a good deal too relaxed according to some, who wish he would learn something from the Protestant work ethic. He is genial and full of charm—the world would soon fall in love with him if he were elected.

And he would have a few enemies, for he would have the curia continue in its present, conservative mold. His written work is rather disappointing—he is no intellectual—but he is a good communicator with a strong voice. (He delivered the De Lubac memorial lecture in Salford, England, in February 1999.) He would be a powerful symbol of the Church of the future, which will move its center of gravity from Europe to the Third World, and perhaps especially to Africa. And his knowledge of Christian-Muslim relations would be important for the future as well.

The name of Bernardin **Gantin** (seventy-seven) has been batted around as an African *papabile* ever since the conclave that elected John Paul I. Though he speaks French, his name is African rather than French (it means "tree of iron"), and it is incorrect to nasalize the two syllables: it is pronounced "Gan-teen." He comes from the small country of Benin, to the west of Nigeria, and became the first black African archbishop of modern times when John XXIII named him to Cotonu archdiocese in 1960. He came to the Vatican in 1971 and has the longest curial experience of any African, moving through three dicasteries. He was made a cardinal back in 1977 by Paul VI, who was generally a good talent scout. Yet he still remains a rather shadowy figure. The general view is that this is because he is something of a token African, but it has also sometimes been suggested that it is because his power is more felt than seen. He was prefect for fourteen years of the Congregation for Bishops—arguably the congregation with the most influence of all for the future of the Church—and in that capacity he met and spoke with the pope almost every week, which is more than almost anyone else in the Curia. He emerged briefly from the shadows when he spoke out against careerism among bishops. He was "very shocked," he said, by bishops who looked for transfers from diocese to diocese as a kind of promotion, and he was in favor of ending the custom of "cardinalate sees," key dioceses (such as Westminster or New York or Los Angeles) in which there is the expectation that the archbishop will be made cardinal. Though these views were first expressed by Cardinal Fagiolo (we slid over him rapidly, as one of the over-eighties), Gantin reinforced his opinions quite forcefully in an interview in the conservative magazine *30 Days* before, once again, sinking into the shadows.

Whatever the judgment of Gantin's abilities, his age now makes him look unlikely. Gantin will have to content himself with chairing the conclave in his role as dean of the college of cardinals.

There is another impressive candidate, but he is almost unknown. Cardinal Christian Wiyghan **Tumi**, archbishop of Douala in Cameroon, is a big man with an even bigger sense of presence. He is respected for his impregnable uprightness and honesty in a world of nepotism and corruption. Indeed, his firmness on points of principle—the iniquity of tribal prejudice, for example, or the importance of Africanization— make him veer to the dictatorial. He throws his weight about on pastoral visitations and dismisses the work of theologians belonging to the Ecumenical Association of Third World Theologians. He studied in France and Switzerland and has been a bishop since 1980 and a cardinal since 1988. He has also been president of the Pan-African bishops' body SECAM (Symposium of Episcopal Conferences of Africa and Madagascar). So he has plenty of experience, even if it is limited to Africa. He just might catch the imagination of the cardinals in the conclave, if they saw his evident stature and did not see his authoritarian side. But it might still feel too big a leap in the dark to entrust the Church into the hands of someone from such a different culture, with all its traditions of tribal chiefs.

Hyacinthe **Thiandoum** (seventy-eight), archbishop of Dakar in Senegal, could be observed at the Synod for Africa, where he was *relator*, and said that an African liturgical rite was not a concession, but a right. He is even older than Gantin without having had his Vatican experience.

The other Africans are more unknown. Under the watershed of seventy-five years we find English-speaking Emmanuel Wamala (seventy-three), cardinal archbishop of Kampala, Uganda; English-speaking Polycarp Pengo (fifty-five), cardinal archbishop of Dar-es-Salaam, Tanzania; French-speaking Frédéric Etsou-Nzabi-Bamungwabi (sixty-nine), cardinal archbishop of Kinshasa, Congo; French-speaking Armand Gaetan Razafindratandra (seventy-four), cardinal archbishop of Antananarivo, Madagascar; and Portuguese-speaking Alexandre do Nascimento (seventy-four), cardinal archbishop of Luanda, Angola. Then, over seventy-five, we find the Ethiopian Paulos Tzadua (seventy-eight), the Kenyan Maurice Michael Otunga (seventy-six), and Alexandre José Maria dos Santos (seventy-five) from Mozambique.

The Asians and Oceanians

Asia is not very fertile territory for looking for a pope. Except in the Philippines, Christians are a minority in Asia, so the sense of confidence and authority needed for a pope is lacking.

What about the Philippines, then? There are three contenders. Cardinal Jaime **Sin** (seventy-one), archbishop of Manila, at least is famous, ever since he played a high-profile role in supporting Cory Aquino's 1986 overthrow of the Marcos regime. But a time of prominence on the national scene is not necessarily the right preparation for being pope. The cardinal archbishop of Cebu, by contrast, Ricardo **Vidal** (sixty-eight), is not known enough to attract votes. He used to be spiritual director in a seminary and is said to be a modest man. Cardinal José **Sánchez** (seventy-nine), formerly prefect of the Congregation for the Clergy, is a great defender of compulsory clerical celibacy. Nothing can faze him—neither the statistics of decline nor Third World demands for a married priesthood on the grounds that "the sacraments are for people." The constant debate about the priesthood and its future, he told a conference on celibacy in May 1993, "only goes to show how towering is the figure of the Catholic priest." Fortunately he is nearly touching eighty.

After the Philippines, India is arguably the most Catholic country of Asia, but all the Indian cardinals are over seventy-five. Cardinal Simon **Lourdusamy** (seventy-five), the retired prefect of Congregation for the Oriental Churches, is the youngest of them. Antony Padiyara (seventy-eight) and Simon Ignatius Pimenta (seventy-nine) are out of the running.

Jesuit Cardinal Paul **Shan Kuo-hsi** (seventy-six), bishop of Kaohsiung in Taiwan, became known internationally when the pope chose him as *relator* for the Synod for Asia and made him a cardinal at the age of seventy-four. He is a soft-spoken, humble, well-educated man, who said, probably correctly, that the choice was a symbol of the pope's solidarity with the persecuted Chinese Church (he spent the first twenty-five years of his life in mainland China). Cardinal John Baptist Wu Cheng-chung (seventy-four) is an exile from China who has lived in the United States and Taiwan before ending up as bishop of Hong Kong. Julius Riyadi Darmaatmadja (sixty-five) is archbishop of Jakarta, Indonesia, and another Jesuit cardinal. Michael Michai Kitbunchu (seventy) is cardinal archbishop of Bangkok, Thailand, and has learned from his Buddhist contacts the importance of peace and of breaking down barriers of discrimination. Peter Seiichi Shirayanagi (seventy-one) is cardinal archbishop of Tokyo, a modest but popular man and another advocate of ecumenical and interreligious dialogue: "In the past, too many human factors have influenced the understanding of the gospel and the way of announcing it," he says. The Korean Stephen Kim Sou-hwan (seventy-seven) is now too old.

Passing through Asia and beyond, we reach Australia and New Zealand. The Australians are probably also too old. Cardinal Edward Bede **Clancy** (seventy-six) is keen not to put a foot wrong with Rome, but falls into the upper-seventies bracket, as does his compatriot Cardinal Edward Idris **Cassidy** (seventy-five), who is a kindly and likable man and has ten years' experience in running the Pontifical Council for Promoting Christian Unity. As ecumenism has slowly drifted into the doldrums, Cassidy has been reduced to traveling the world talking about the importance of local ecumenism—a sure sign that the "big picture" wasn't playing very well. He had only a minor role in the "welcome" extended to dissident Anglicans who could not stomach women priests and generally, in serious matters, has to play second fiddle to Cardinal Ratzinger. Cassidy might be an acceptable compromise candidate, a mild and safe man who has the relevant experience and is more of an executive than an innovator, but his age is now against him.

New Zealand brings Thomas Stafford **Williams** (sixty-nine), archbishop of Wellington, who has a good knowledge of the remote and interesting islands in the Pacific Ocean and who did a good job as copresident at the Synod for Oceania. But valuable as the Pacific experience is for the wider Church, it may be thought too particular an experience to provide sufficient basis for a future papacy. For the same reason, and also because of age, Cardinal Pio Taofinu'u (seventy-six) from the Pacific island of Samoa would be a most unlikely choice.

The Not-Yet-Cardinals

At this point we may feel like breathing a huge sigh of relief for having reached the end of the list. But we must not forget that another consistory would raise the numbers again, and one could drop on us at any moment. Indeed a consistory for the new millennium is just the sort of idea likely to appeal to John Paul II. So we need to devote a moment's consideration to those who are likely to be among the next batch of cardinals. We cannot predict everyone on such a list, but we can have a pretty shrewd guess at some of them.

Vietnamese Archbishop François Xavier **Nguyen Van Thuan** (seventy-one) is now president of the Pontifical Council for Justice and Peace, succeeding Cardinal Etchegaray. Once made a cardinal, as is natural (but not automatic) for someone in that job, he could become a convincing candidate for the papacy. His main strength is holiness, having been imprisoned for thirteen years, nine of them in solitary confinement. He has written beautiful spiritual books out of the deprivation and suffering he endured, and, if the conclave wanted both continuity with and difference from, the old regime, Van Thuan would be a compelling choice. His style could not be more different from Wojtyla's—shy, modest, gentle, introverted, reluctant to criticize—but his message would be a similar one—the importance of the gospel for a godless world. But because of his tentativeness, a vote for Van Thuan could be a vote for more control than ever before by the bad boys of the Curia.

Another Asian head of a Vatican dicastery is Japanese Bishop Stephen **Hamao** (sixty-nine), made president of the relatively insignificant Pontifical Council for the Pastoral Care of Migrants and Itinerants, after the Synod for Asia complained that there should be more Asians in the Curia. He is a very open man, not at all the sort you expect to find

in the Vatican, but he is settling in to his new life with a positive attitude. There is no particular reason why he should be
made a cardinal just because he heads one of the more
obscure councils, but also no reason why he should not be
one, if the pope is looking for more talent from the East.

Another Asian who looks a good bet for promotion is
Archbishop Thomas **Menamparampil** (sixty-three) of Guwa-
hati in India, whose talents were evident at the Synod for
Asia. Though unthreatening to the Vatican system in his attitudes, he is a highly educated man—originally from Kerala,
home the cultural elite of India—and has exceptional talent
as a writer. He also has a genuinely deep spirituality. Perhaps
a job in Rome will come his way soon, and at some stage a
cardinal's hat.

Archbishop Cláudio **Hummes** (sixty-five) has succeeded
Cardinal Arns in São Paulo, one of the most important dioceses in Brazil and, indeed, in the world. Though Hummes
is generally classed as a conservative, he used to be a progressive, so at least he has some depth of experience. Since
taking over, he has made a clear stand on some human
rights issues (torture, homelessness), although his general
approach is to avoid engaging the social struggle and to
take a greater interest in charismatic prayer. He is a man
who is expected to be given more responsibilities.

From the archdiocese of Tegucigalpa in Honduras is a
quite exceptional bishop, still quite young and with packs of
energy, called Oscar **Rodríguez Maradiaga** (fifty-seven). Not
the sort who gets promoted these days, one might think, but
Rodríguez Maradiaga is already a member of several Vatican
dicasteries and was one of John Paul II's own nominees to
the postsynodal council after the Synod for America. He is
so articulate he can play his cards in several ways, depending
on the need of the moment, but at the same time he is
refreshingly honest and outspoken. Until recently he was

president of CELAM, and he was one of the small group who met Gerhard Schröder, the German chancellor, at the G7 meeting in Cologne to hand over the Jubilee 2000 petition. He is a good linguist and could go a very long way. Not quite pope this time around, however.

From the United States, Archbishop Justin Francis **Rigali** (sixty-four) of St. Louis is an obvious candidate to be made cardinal. He has some two decades of Roman experience and was secretary to the Congregation for Bishops before going to St. Louis in 1994. If he were a cardinal, he might be *papabile*. Apart from coming from the United States, that is.

We do not yet (as we go to press) know the name of the new archbishop of Westminster. But traditionally this post carries a cardinal's hat, despite the attempts by Gantin and Fagiolo to change the system. Irish archbishop Sean **Brady** (sixty) may also become a cardinal, like his predecessor at Armagh, Cahal Daly. Another diocese that traditionally brings a cardinal's hat is Santiago de Chile, where Francisco Javier **Errázuriz Ossa** (sixty-six) was appointed in 1998 after a determined campaign of opposition to the appointment of a conservative who was close to the military.

Conclusion

So many candidates, and yet no one is quite right. Schönborn looks a strong candidate, but at fifty-four has alarmingly long to live. The other top candidates—whether conservatives or moderates—are all over seventy, but could still get in as a temporary solution: Martini for his vision, Ratzinger for his brains, Biffi for his tenacity, Moreira Neves for his experience, Cé for his patience, Piovanelli for his dialogue, Van Thuan for his holiness. The candidates in their sixties—the ideal age—are mostly outsiders and something of a risk: Arinze the African, Turcotte the Canadian,

Winning the Scot, Mahony of the United States. Poupard of France has enough experience of the Curia, but seems to lack a following. Rouco Varela of Spain has plenty of admirers within Spain, but has no experience of the Curia and is little known outside his own country. Then, despite being that little bit younger, there are the candidates under seventy who breathe a depressingly preconciliar air: Castrillón the conservative, Tettamanzi the dull.

What we can say with more confidence is that a number of men will go into the conclave very well qualified for the job and come out having gotten no further than the role of kingmaker, having failed to project sufficiently that all-important quality of "man of God." Among them we expect: López Trujillo, Sodano, Schotte, Pio Laghi, Tomko, Medina Estévez, Ruini.

But someone we have looked at must surely get the job. It will not be a real progressive, for there are not any progressives among the cardinals. But there are intelligent moderates who could open up some of the avenues that have been blocked by John Paul II on centralization, collegiality, dialogue, theological freedom, and the role of laity. Some cardinals will want this, and if they win the day, we could see a pope like Martini, Danneels, Turcotte, or Mahony. Any of these would bring hopes of change in the Church.

But others in the college will be keen to preserve the firm lines of John Paul's traditionalist papacy. They will recognize the need for a pope of a different style, but will not countenance electing a pope of different policies. Their favorites might be Ratzinger, Castrillón, Boffi, or Rouco Varela. With any of these, John Paul's conservative legacy should remain quite safe.

Or the cardinals might go for someone less identified with right or left, someone chosen for qualities other than his Church politics. Being pope can open up a man in the most amazing ways, as the world saw with John XXIII. Hope springs eternal in the Catholic breast that the Holy Spirit will give another such surprise to the Church. Such hopes could be fixed on men like Schönborn, Tettamanzi, or Arinze, all of whom are clearly conservatives now, but who have sufficient charm that the world could well fall in love with one of them and pin their hopes on him.

The crowds who watch for the color of the smoke at the end of each electoral day may come initially out of curiosity, but it is not long before their fascination will give way to hope. When the white smoke appears, there will be no words for the excitement and anticipation. People will converge from all directions in the thousands to be within sight of that tiny, distant balcony at that dramatic, historic moment when they hear the well-known words *habemus papam* ("We have a pope"). And then the name will come, and they will turn to their neighbor and say, "Who?"

Good, bad, or indifferent, the man who comes out in his new, white soutane will be the key to the Church's continuity with both past and future. He will be the successor to St. Peter, the first Bishop of Rome. And he will be the channel of hope, however tenuous, that the Church may move just a little closer to the reign of God.

NOTES

Prelude

1. Giovanni XXIII, *Quindici Letture,* edited by Loris F. Capovilla (Rome: Storia e letterature, 1970), p. 481.

Chapter 1

1. Timothy Tindal-Robertson, *Fátima, Russia and Pope John Paul II* (Cambridge, MA: Ravengate Press, 1992), p. 47.

2. Patrick du Laubier, *Sociologie de l'Eglise Catholique* (Fribourg: Editions universitaires, 1993), p. 47. Three other popes were forced to abdicate, which is not good precedent for a voluntary abdication: Silverius in 537, John XVIII in 1009, and Gregory XII in 1415. See J. D. N. Kelly, *The Oxford Dictionary of the Popes* (Oxford: Oxford University Press, 1989).

3. Jean Chélini, *Au Vatican de Jean-Paul II* (Paris: Hachette, 1985), p. 279.

4. Giancarlo Zizola, *Quale Papa?* (Rome: Borla, 1977).

5. *The Tablet,* June 19, 1993, p. 799.

6. Review of M. Menzo, *Papa Giovanni vescovo di Roma* (Cinisello: Paoline, 1991), in *Cristianesimo nella storia* 14 (1993), p. 92.

Chapter 2

1. John F. Brodrick, S.J., "The Sacred College of Cardinals, Size and Geographical Composition (1099–1986)," in *Archivum Historiae Pontificiae,* p. 10.

2. Chateaubriand is usually thought of as a conservative thinker because he was opposed to the Enlightenment. But in his preface to *Le Génie du Christianisme* he said that if the book were to be rewritten, he would stress not so much the benefits of religion in the past as "Christianity as the thought of the future and of human freedom." That brought him closer to Lammenais.

3. Margaret Pawley, *Faith and Family: The Life and Circle of Ambrose Philipps de Lisle* (Norwich: Canterbury Press, 1991), p. 42.

4. Giancarlo Zizola, *Quale Papa?* (Rome: Borla, 1977), pp. 135–36.

5. Gerald P. Fogarty, S.J., *The Vatican and the American Hierarchy from 1870 to 1965* (Michael Glazier, 1985), p. 206.

6. Peter Hebblethwaite, *Paul VI: The First Modern Pope* (New York: Paulist Press, 1993), p. 128.

7. Zizola, *Quale Papa?* p. 138.

8. Fogarty, *The Vatican and the American Hierarchy,* p. 218. O'Connell argued with Cardinal Pietro Gasparri, *camerlengo,* that he should either have given the Americans "some warning of Benedict's failing health or delayed the conclave to give them time to arrive" (p. 219).

9. Hebblethwaite, *Paul VI,* p. 134.

10. Fogarty, *The Vatican and the American Hierarchy,* p. 257.

11. Alberto Melloni, *"Governi e diplomazie davanti all'annuncio del Vaticano II,"* in *A la Veille de Vatican II,* edited by M. Lamberigts and Cl. Soetens (Leuven, 1992), p. 221.

12. Peter Hebblethwaite, *John XXIII: Shepherd of the Modern World* (New York: Doubleday, 1985), p. 282. A full account is contained in chap. 12, "1958: The Wide-Open Conclave."

13. Loris F. Capovilla, ed., *Lettere ai Familiari,* II, 1968, p. 368.

14. John Cooney, *The American Pope: The Life and Times of Francis Cardinal Spellman* (New York: Times Books, 1984), p. 258.

15. Rome Report, 72, June 6, 1963, unpublished, Canterbury Cathedral Archives.

Chapter 3

1. Giancarlo Zizola, *Microfono di Dio*, p. 232. St. John Lateran is the cathedral church of the bishop of Rome, and popes lived in the Lateran Palace until 1367 (when they were not in Avignon). St. Peter's belongs to all Christian peoples.

2. Peter Hebblethwaite, *Paul VI: The First Modern Pope* (New York: Paulist Press, 1993), p. 590.

3. Ibid., p. 591.

4. Giancarlo Zizola, *Quale Papa?* (Rome: Borla, 1977), p. 87.

5. Benny Lai, *Les Secrets du Vatican,* p. 172.

6. George A. Schlichte, *Politics in the Purple Kingdom: The Derailment of Vatican II* (Kansas City, MO: Sheed and Ward, 1993), pp. 62–63.

7. Denis E. Hurley, letter to Peter Hebblethwaite, June 22, 1993.

8. Benny Lai, *Il Papa non eletto,* p. 264.

9. John Cornwell, *A Thief in the Night* (New York: Simon & Schuster, 1989), p. 265.

10. For this suggestion, see Lai, *Il Papa non eletto,* p. 273.

11. Ibid., p. 278.

12. Ibid., p. 279.

13. Giancarlo Zizola: *Il Conclave: storia e segreti* (Rome: Newton Compton Editori, 1993), p. 307.

Chapter 4

1. Jas Gawronski, "Io, il Papa tra l'Ovest e l'Est," *La Stampa,* November 2, 1993.

2. René Luneau and Paul Ladrière, eds., *Le Rêve de Compostelle* (Paris: Centurion, 1989), p. 153.

3. John Whale, ed., *The Pope from Poland: An Assessment* (London: Collins, 1980), p. 143.

4. Luneau and Ladrière, *Le Rêve,* pp. 15–16.

5. Ibid., p. 16.

6. Ibid., p. 28 (Strasbourg, October 11, 1988).

7. Quoted in Theo Mechtenberg, "Wie Katholisch Ist das Katholische Polen?" in *Orientierung,* February 15, 1993, p. 27.

Chapter 5

1. *Independent* magazine, October 10, 1993, p. 50.

2. *Spectator,* March 5, 1994, p. 27.

3. *New York Times*, August 8, 1993, reviewing Peter Hebblethwaite's *Paul VI* and David Willey's *God's Politician*.

4. "Can Women Be Priests?" in *Origins*, July 1, 1976, pp. 92–96.

5. Interview with John Cornwell, *Sunday Times* magazine, April 25, 1993.

6. Ladislas Orsy, S.J., "How to Relate Theology and Canon Law," in *Origins* 22, January 21, 1993.

Chapter 6

1. Patrick du Laubier, *Sociologie de l'Eglise Catholique* (Fribourg: Editions universitaires, 1993). But methods of counting popes vary. Richard McBrien, in the *Encyclopedia of Catholicism* (San Francisco: HarperSanFrancisco, 1995) and *Lives of the Popes* (San Francisco: HarperSanFrancisco, 1997), says that the next pope will be the 263rd. Eamon Duffy, in *Saints and Sinners: A History of the Popes* (New Haven: Yale University Press, 1997), says the 262nd.

2. Background information on Hadrian VI is taken from E. Halkin, *Adrien VI et la réforme de l'Eglise,* in *Eph. Theol. Lovanienses* (1959); C. Burmann, *Hadrianus VI sive analecta historica de Hadriano Sexto* (Utrecht, 1727); Paulius Jovius, *Vita;* Ludwig Pastor, *History of the Popes,* vol. IX (London, 1910); and Angelo Mercati, *Dall' Archivo Vaticano,* Diarii di concistori del Ponificato di Adriano VI, Studi e testi 157 (Vatican, 1951).

Chapter 7

1. Carlo Maria Martini, quoted in "A Pastor's Vision," an interview with Gerard O'Connell, *Tablet,* July 10, 1993, p. 878.

2. "Mahony Is a Big Man in the Church," interview with Arthur Jones, *National Catholic Reporter,* November 12, 1993.

3. See Francis McDonagh, in *The Challenges for the Latin American Church* (London: Catholic Institute for International Relations, 1993), p. 11.

4. Ibid., p. 14.

5. Penny Lernoux, "Feared Latin Prelate Moving Towards Papacy," *National Catholic Reporter,* September 9, 1993, p. 24.

INDEX